Surviving Serendipity

Surviving Serendipity

A Memoir

Written By
Lawrence J. Enders, M.D.

Copyright © 2011 by Lawrence J. Enders, M.D..

Library of Congress Control Number: 2011905878
ISBN: Hardcover   978-1-4628-5667-1
           Softcover   978-1-4628-5666-4
           Ebook   978-1-4628-5668-8

All rights reserved. No part of this book may be reproduced or transmitted in any form or by any means, electronic or mechanical, including photocopying, recording, or by any information storage and retrieval system, without permission in writing from the copyright owner.

This book was printed in the United States of America.

To order additional copies of this book, contact:
Xlibris Corporation
1-888-795-4274
www.Xlibris.com
Orders@Xlibris.com
97890

Contents

Chapter 1:	Now That's Poor Planning	1
Chapter 2:	Have I Got A Deal For You!	5
Chapter 3:	Have I Got Another Deal For You!	10
Chapter 4:	What Goes Up Must Come Down	13
Chapter 5:	It's All Up In The Air	16
Chapter 6:	No Jumping, Please!	22
Chapter 7:	Oh, 'Chute!	26
Chapter 8:	This Is Surviving?	31
Chapter 9:	This Is The Pits!	35
Chapter 10:	The Gravity Of It All	45
Chapter 11:	A-Wackies & Bubbles	50
Chapter 12:	Swinging On A String	61
Chapter 13:	Spacemen & Pilots & Presidents, Oh My!	70
Chapter 14:	Astronauts Are Only Human	76
Chapter 15:	There Really Isn't A Candy-Striped Pole Up There?	83
Chapter 16:	A Real Fly-By-Night Outfit	92
Chapter 17:	Oh, Rats!	95

Chapter 18:	A Guy Could Get Hurt Doing This!	106
Chapter 19:	Back In The Saddle Again	116
Chapter 20:	Too Tall Joe Or Just Don't Close The Hatch	121
Chapter 21:	Puddle Jumping The Pacific	123
Chapter 22:	Educating A Bird	129
Chapter 23:	Not With *My* Dog!	133
Chapter 24:	A Smash With M*A*S*H	139
Chapter 25:	A Hole In My Heart	145
Chapter 26:	Doc-In-Demand	147
Chapter 27:	"Dining In" / "Dining Out"	150
Chapter 28:	Generals & Germans & G-Men, Oh My!	159
Chapter 29:	More Vodka, Please!	166
Chapter 30:	Have I Got A Deal For You—Part 3	174
Chapter 31:	Doctor Who?	183
Chapter 32:	Tales Of Trials	185
Chapter 33:	Causes & Correlations	193
Chapter 34:	Did You Find the "Yet" Yet?	196

Dedication

"To all the members of my family—especially those who endured the consequences of a lifestyle which made this book possible."

Preface

This semblance of an "autobiography" was prompted by friends and family who were mesmerized by the amazing number of "serendipitous" events which so frequently dotted my life.

I personally believe that most people have experienced some similar happenings. In my case, these happenings just seemed so remotely unlikely for someone whose original goal in life was to be a very stable, home-town physician. As the story will reveal, what actually transpired was a far cry from that! Unusual incidents and unusual people became the usual.

The events in this book are real. They happened as they are portrayed, to the best of my recollections. The sequence of events is reasonably, chronologically correct. What was of enormous help was my considerable collection of memorabilia for me to reference.

The names and places are all real, with the exceptions of the FBI Agent and my three Russian KGB acquaintances. Since I believe they are all still alive, it is prudent to not reveal their identities.

I hope you will find these unusual, albeit real, experiences interesting.

Lawrence J. Enders, MD, MPH, FACPM
December, 2010

1

~ Now That's Poor Planning ~

According to *Webster's New World Dictionary*, Second College Edition, the word **SERENDIPITY** includes the following definition:

'an apparent aptitude for making fortunate discoveries accidentally'

Well, this sums up a great deal of my life, particularly the 23 years I spent in the US Air Force as a Flight Surgeon. Let me begin with this observation. Many people believe they have control over their own lives, at least once they "fly the coop" and are out from under parental influence. We know that life has its ups and downs but surely our future is in our own hands, right?

I now have a very different take on that. True, in any given situation it's our individual choice to do what is "right" or "wrong," to say "yes" or "no." But is one person's "right" *always* right? Or is one person's "wrong" *always* wrong? From nowhere a situation can evolve which somehow results in you coming out all the better for it. Were you in any way involved in its creation, or was the whole of it simply this thing called "Serendipity?"

Do I believe the attitude that "coming out smelling like a rose" plays a much larger part in our lives than we would want to admit? Yes, I believe it does, and I can speak to that fact—to a great degree—because that sums up the story of my life.

It is not uncommon that many teenagers have youthful "delusions of grandeur" in which they believe they will become a rock star, a country western singer, a famous race car driver, or a sportsman of extraordinary talent. They may even envision themselves winning a Nobel Prize for some outstanding discovery or perhaps becoming a great statesman!

Then as they grow up and mature a little, they begin to realize the amount of sweat, personal inconvenience, hard work and dedication any of these goals require. They then become more "practical." They get some education, a job, the girl of their dreams, a nice house and a mortgage. They settle down to raise their children. And good for them, as there's absolutely nothing wrong with being "normal" in this great country of ours.

I was born in a middle-class suburb of a good-sized city in Minnesota. One of my parents' goals was that I get a better education than they had. They struggled financially to send me to good schools, and at these schools my values and personality were significantly influenced. First by the Notre Dame Nuns, and then by the Christian Brothers who also ran the Military Academy where I spent grades nine through twelve. From them I learned two powerful things, guilt and discipline! For example, I was absolutely certain that if I ate meat on Friday, I would almost instantly be struck by lightning and forever become a crispy critter in that Valhalla beneath the ground!

In the Military Academy, I learned their brand of discipline which helped me focus on what was most important to me at that time . . . education! My high school grades were quite respectable and facilitated my acceptance into a Jesuit University in a neighboring state.

Hard work, some part-time jobs, and academic perseverance subsequently resulted in my acceptance into medical school. There you are. Now was that not, pretty much, me controlling my life? Additionally I was facilitating a dream which my parents had so long and quietly envisioned, "Our son, the Doctor," and their joy of seeing me practice in our home town where every day they could admire my shingle.

Alas, that was not to be!

Medical school was tough—and costly. Also, I married during this period. My wife worked, and I worked part-time in the evenings as a clothing salesman and on weekends as a spray painter at a boat trailer assembly plant. This was the period where my "guilt training" kicked in. I was conditioned to the fact that the only acceptable form of birth control was the infamous Rhythm Method and, of course, that produced a family for us.

Now rhythm is a good thing, especially if it is associated with controlling your heartbeat, or keeping time with music, or on a dance floor. Let me tell you, in bed it's pretty ineffective! Nevertheless, we persevered and I completed medical school, receiving my M.D.

Now in order to get a license to actually practice medicine, what most states require, in addition to your M.D., is a one-year internship. That entails working in a hospital on a variety of services under the tutelage of staff doctors and private practitioners who have privileges in that hospital. Although I was an M.D. and could legally treat and prescribe, the patients "belonged" to another doctor. I was basically their assistant. Some of the practicing doctors were really very generous in letting me handle their patients, and ironically this seemed to be especially so around the hours of two and three o'clock in the morning!

On the OB (Obstetrics) Service, I personally delivered about two hundred babies, sometimes guided by the patient's doctor, and sometimes on my own when the private M.D. couldn't make it into the hospital in time (usually in the wee hours of the morning). During the three months I was on OB, my schedule was "on duty for thirty-six hours, off duty for twelve" which didn't leave much time for the family. Mostly, it was a very happy experience, with new babies and delighted parents. I even witnessed a couple of "immaculate conceptions" during my time there.

Case in point: One particular night, a 22-year-old woman brought her younger sister, maybe 16 years old, into the emergency room. The chief complaint of the younger girl was (and I quote), "a sudden onset of diarrhea" to the extent that it was running down her legs. I examined the girl and immediately recognized that the "diarrhea" was actually amniotic fluid. That's the fluid in which a fetus floats inside a pregnant uterus. Her water had broken.

I called her sister over and explained to her that her baby sister would soon be delivering a baby. The older sibling asked to have a few minutes alone with her sister. After about five minutes, she came back into the room and pronounced that I had obviously misdiagnosed the situation as the young girl had sworn that she had "never had relations with a man." There you go. It's amazing what a person can pick up off a toilet seat!

Five hours later I delivered my first and only case of parthenogenesis, all seven pounds twelve ounces of him. Parthenogenesis is described in *Dorland's Medical Dictionary* as a "modified form of sexual reproduction for the development of the gamete (which is the egg) without fertilization." It occurs in some plants, in arthropods, honey bees, and wasps. Later, I checked the admission sheet and found that, sure enough, she was a *White Anglo Saxon Protestant*—a WASP! Situation explained.

Being in control of my life as I was, it seemed that a residency to become a OB/GYN specialist was looming very brightly in my future.

Enter Serendipity.

2

~ Have I Got A Deal For You! ~

Very near the end of my internship, I went down to the interns' quarters one day only to find a man standing there. Looking well-dressed and very official, he asked if I was Doctor Enders. I told him I was. This was back in the days when all U.S. males were required to register for the military draft at age eighteen. I had done so at that age of course, but now, after university, medical school, an internship, and all the other things that had occurred in my life, I had totally forgotten anything I had signed six years previously.

But here was this man asking me if I was, indeed, Doctor Enders.

He said, "Okay, doctor, you may remember signing the required papers for the draft when you were eighteen. Well, Uncle Sam wants you now." He continued, "But we are going to give you a choice. Should you choose to go into a specialty, we'll defer you for several more years to complete your residency. You may even be able to start a practice. But when we need you, we will take you and put you wherever we want, in whatever branch of the service we want."

"But first, have I got a deal for you! Consider this: You can come in now, pick your branch of service, get your two years out of the way, and then go about your life without further interference."

Well, that was a no-brainer for me. I certainly wasn't going to establish myself in a residency and set up a practice, only to be pulled out of it to be a something, somewhere, in some branch of the service. If Uncle Sam wanted me, better now than at some inconvenient time in the future . . . one that I was so sure I was controlling.

I told him I preferred to go into the Air Force and that I wanted to go into Flight Surgeon's School. I had always been interested in airplanes. I had actually been up a few times in light aircraft and was completely mesmerized by being in the sky.

Well, they didn't waste much time processing me. Three months after making that momentous decision, I reported to Randolph Air Force Base as a brand new First Lieutenant and was enrolled in the School of Aviation Medicine (as it was known at that time). A few years later, the new facility would be called the School of Aerospace Medicine.

I was to take their six-week course in Flight Medicine, which was the basic flight surgeons' course. On completion, I would be designated as an aeromedical examiner for one year. In the academic portion, you learned enough to identify any medical problems resulting from flying, as well as understanding those illnesses which could preclude a pilot from flying safely.

"The School of Aviation Medicine in 1957"

Regardless of title, I was still virtually only a passenger with the pilots. If you asked, and they had room for you, they would take you up on whatever mission they were tasked with for that day. Sometimes, if you were lucky and the pilot trusted you, he might even give you some stick time during the flight.

One interesting thing is that I basically had two jobs during those first compulsory years in the Air Force. My primary job was, of course, to take care of the pilots and air crews, and to fly with them whenever possible. The second "job" was to do the entrance physical examinations for all the new Flight Nurses coming into the Air Force. There were many of my friends who seemed to think that maybe—just maybe—I had the best damned job in the Air Force at that time.

But, that's a whole other story.

I had good rapport with the air crew members and, because they liked me, I got to fly with them pretty often. One such opportunity occurred when the Flight Safety Officer at Maxwell Air Force Base asked me if I wanted to go on a flight with him in a T-33. I jumped at that, as the T-33 is a little two-seater jet, and that meant he'd let me have some stick time. He said, "Doc, we're both going to get some cross-country navigational time."

As an Air Force flight crew member, one has to log in a certain number of hours under various types of flight conditions. In addition to the relatively simple "up in the air, fly around town and come down" flights, one needed night flights and a certain number of flights that were in real or simulated weather.

When the visibility outside the aircraft is totally obscured, the pilot must fly on instruments alone, so these are called instrument flights. If there were no clouds about to produce this situation, visibility can be artificially obscured by a hood inside the aircraft canopy. Slide this opaque hood forward and the pilot can see nothing outside the aircraft, thereby again producing the need to rely solely on his instruments to get him where he needs to be at the time he needs to be there.

The fourth requirement was periodic cross-country navigational flights. It's one thing to get in the air a few thousand feet and fly around in an area where you can identify all kinds of landmarks visually. It is an entirely different matter to fly to an unfamiliar destination at some thirty-odd thousand feet, where you cannot distinguish any reference points on the ground, and make it with confidence.

This skill set requires you to follow your charts, relying on your instruments as you fly to one location, then on to a second and maybe even a third point, and so on, until you arrive at your final destination—and not get lost along the way!

So my friendly safety officer was going to do this particular cross-country navigational flight to the town of Douglas, Arizona, where there was a very small airfield. At the time I wondered how he intended to land a jet aircraft onto such a short runway! But the T-33 itself was a relatively small plane compared to some jets, and it had decent power.

It turned out that the reason we were going to Douglas, Arizona, was because it was just across the border from the Mexican town of Agua Prieta. That town was a little "secret" among the pilots at the base. There was a beat up old Jeep set aside at that airport for the use of the Air Force pilots. The border guard was one sleepy old guy who asked very few questions when you crossed into Mexico, and none at all when you came back. Tips were greatly appreciated. What we brought back this time was Oso Negro 100-proof gin. I think that amounted to four very large bottles. The cost? Just over $3.00 each!

Now, the T-33 was not designed to carry cargo. You cannot put anything inside the cockpit for obvious reasons—you don't want anything interfering with your feet, the controls, or with the ejection system in case you had to leave in a hurry.

But pilot ingenuity had an answer. Up in the nose of the T-33, where the radio equipment was housed, there is a bit of open space. Mind you, that "nose space" was *not* pressurized. But we were able to stack the four bottles of gin there in a somewhat suitable manner. Because that space was not pressurized, we had to make sure that our return home flight plan would not take us to altitudes above twelve or thirteen thousand feet. Flying at a higher altitude would dramatically lower the atmospheric pressure outside of a vessel (i.e., a bottle) causing the air inside to expand. As luck would have it, on our way back to our base in Alabama, we encountered thunderstorm activity, forcing us to climb to about twenty-five thousand feet.

Of course, we had no idea what was happening inside the nose of our T-33 until we landed. The crew chief was waiting for us so he could post-flight the aircraft. As we opened the canopy, we could hear him cussing a blue streak—words probably best left unsaid here. Actually, the situation was much worse. It turned out that all of our bottles had burst from the expanding pressure inside them, spewing the precious contents over the radio equipment and dripping down onto the parking ramp.

We had wondered why our radio equipment did not appear to be working to specification on the journey home! I suppose if you are inundated with about four bottles of 100-proof gin you might not perform as you should either!

3

~ Have I Got Another Deal For You! ~

Mind you, not everything was fun during those first couple of years. There were lots of ups and downs, good days and bad. Here is an example of a *very* bad day.

As the Flight Surgeon on duty, I was called out late one afternoon and directed to go to a civilian airfield on the other side of town from my base. There, the Alabama National Guard was flying some older F-84 Thunderbirds. The F-84 was a very, very heavy plane and it needed a great deal of power and a long roll to get airborne. It had rained the day before and all the land around the runway was muddy.

The pilot did his long roll but the aircraft lost power right after lift off. The plane impacted about two thousand yards off the end of the runway. When the Thunderbird, heavy as it was, hit the mud, it almost stopped dead in its tracks. However, the engine, which was located above and behind the pilot, kept going. It broke free of its mountings and went through the cockpit, decapitating the pilot. Of course there was a fire and the plane was pretty well burned. By the time I got there, the fire department and crash crews had just about extinguished the flames.

A fireman and I, one on each side of the cockpit, climbed onto what remained of the wings and found the body of the pilot from the neck down still strapped into his seat. But he was burned to a crisp, literally. They didn't find his head until much later far down the field near where the engine had come to rest.

Inevitably, members of the press were gathering taking videos and readying reports on the tragedy for the evening news broadcasts. It appeared we were being filmed as we worked to extract the pilot. I believe that on one of the news clips, I had just reached in one side of the cockpit, as had the fireman on the other side, trying to lift the body of the pilot. Because the remains were so completely charred, as I pulled on the upper arm it separated from the shoulder. Not a very happy experience, and I hope to hell the family of that unfortunate man did not watch the news that night.

My two years went by pretty fast, all things considered. Then just before I was due to complete my compulsory time and go back to being a doctor on "civvy street," my boss (a full Colonel in command of the hospital) said to me, "Before you make up your mind to leave us, have I got a deal for you!"

He then told me about this program which was available to me if I chose to remain in the service of Uncle Sam. He said, "I know you like flying. I looked at your records and saw you have more air time than most flight surgeons who are doing their compulsory time. If you want to take a residency in aerospace medicine, here's how we'll do it for you. The government will pay for the whole thing. What I'm saying is that you'll get paid as due your rank, with a generous housing allowance and a subsistence allowance. This residency has four parts." *My ears were well-pricked by this time.*

"The four parts are as follows:

1. We will send you to the University of California, Harvard, or Johns Hopkins to get your Master's Degree in Public Health. That will take one academic year.
2. Following your master's, you'll be sent to Flight School to learn to fly jets.

3. You will then attend the new School of Aerospace Medicine (it was at that time still being built) for a year to study the academics of aerospace medicine along with the hands-on training that goes with all the associated equipment (Centrifuge, Ejection Seats, Parachute Training, Survival Training, Hyperbaric Chambers, etc.).
4. In your final year you will train under a preceptor who is also board certified in Aerospace Medicine.

And again, for those three years we will pay you fully with all the allowances—you're going to love it!"

I considered it for a full thirty-seconds or so, loved the sound of it all, and nodded. Serendipity was again in full swing in my life.

4

~ What Goes Up Must Come Down ~

There were, however, three other incidents during my second year of service which could have sidelined me from any thoughts of continuing to fly.

I only had one sibling, a sister two years older than me, back in Minnesota. She and her husband, Jack, were married, when she was eighteen. Jack owned a small produce company that sold and distributed fruit and vegetables to retail food stores and resorts in Minnesota and Wisconsin. One rather rainy day, Jack was in Rochester, Minnesota, on business and made a last-minute decision to fly from there to Milwaukee to conduct further business.

The commercial airlines had canceled their flights due to bad weather conditions. Nevertheless, Jack, determined to get to Milwaukee as planned, chartered a small twin-engine aircraft from a local pilot. Another man who heard of the charter joined the flight.

The aircraft encountered thunderstorms with severe turbulence along the route. It somehow got into a flat spin from which the pilot was not able to recover. It crashed in a field killing all on board and leaving my twenty-nine year old sister a widow with five small children, ages one to ten.

I needed to log more cross-country flight time. My trip to the funeral in Minnesota could also fulfill this requirement if I traveled by military plane. Calling my safety officer friend, I explained my needs and he was agreeable to accompany me. We checked out a T-33 which got us from Alabama to Minnesota in just two hours. Our base was expecting the aircraft back in forty-eight hours.

Needless to say, I was pretty distraught on the flight back. The first hour was routine, and my mind was drifting to family matters; but my attention sharpened when we were advised there were thunderstorms on our approach route. We were cruising at thirty thousand feet, well above the cloud deck; but we had to come down through it to land. We started our descent about seventy miles out. About forty miles out we entered the clouds and went to instrument flying. Ten miles out and at about eight thousand feet, we encountered moderate turbulence and rain. On the final leg to our landing a wind shear hit us at about six hundred feet.

We were doing about two-hundred fifty mph when our right wing was pushed down hard by the unexpected gust, and we found ourselves completely on our side, one wing down, the other straight up. We had to take immediate action as we had lost all lift and were losing altitude rapidly. We went with the wind and put the stick hard right, threw in a bit of rudder, and completed a full roll to bring us back to straight and level. Our altitude was now about three-hundred fifty feet. We had just done a tight barrel roll on final approach! Throttling back, we were on the ground about forty seconds later. It was decided not to mention this to anyone.

Was Someone "up there" talking to me?

Just a few months later my boss, a senior flight surgeon, was getting in some of his cross-country time in a small, twin-engine prop plane. On the way back to our base, the weather had turned bad and heavy fog had set in. Our runways were closed and the Beechcraft was diverted to an airfield in northern Alabama.

As they approached the civilian airfield, the cloud bank there settled lower. Attempting an instrument landing, the plane crashed on a high, blanketed knoll just short of the runway. My boss was critically injured and burned by the ensuing fire. He spent the next three months in a regional medical center to treat the compound leg fractures, other fractures, and to complete the skin grafts for the burns on his upper arms, chest, and face.

When I finally saw my CO, he was walking stiff-legged and with a cane. His upper body burn scars were still bright red. It was obvious to me he'd never be on flying status again.

I thought of the F-84 pilot, my brother-in-law, my flight back after his funeral, and my boss. I could almost imagine seeing the clouds above my head parting, a lightning bolt coming down, and a loud voice saying, "Hey, man, you're just not getting the message, are you?" I now clearly understood that weather could be a pilot's greatest danger. Sometimes when I hear thunder it's almost like the Almighty saying, "I put you on the Earth, and I can take you off of it anytime I want!"

Warning voices notwithstanding, I continued with my career plans.

5

~ It's All Up In The Air ~

Driving a family of seven, plus a dog, from Montgomery, Alabama, to San Francisco really would test the sanity of anybody! Fortunately, we survived the long drive and arrived at our destination safe and sound. In Berkeley we found a small home which was within walking distance of the University of California where I was to spend the next ten months. This was a time when "panty-raids" and "bra burnings" were popular pastimes, but not at my house. Time passed and we made a family trip to the Napa Valley before I pocketed my MPH (Master's Degree in Public Health). It was then time to head to San Antonio and Flight Training.

Flight School was great! The first several weeks of ground school covered all the basics of the primary subjects like Aerodynamics, Control Systems, Navigation, Charts, Radio Operation, and many more. Then we moved on to the actual flying. T-33 #TR-385 was my bird.

My T-33

From the beginning, the instructor took the back seat and I spent weeks of take-offs, landings, formation flying, aerobatics with barrel rolls, loops, chandelles, and lazy eights. That was followed by navigational exercises, including cross-country flights. It could not have been better! On completion of flight training, I was qualified to handle the aircraft, but because my primary military assignments were medical, I was not allowed to take a plane up by myself. I was required to be accompanied by another qualified pilot—one whose regular job was flying.

I expected the academics at the new School of Aerospace Medicine to be pretty mundane, but I couldn't have been more wrong. "Classroom stuff" may be "classroom stuff," but the hands-on training was spectacular! That's both good news and bad news.

There were ten of us: two Jims, a Myron, a George, a Howie, a Chuck, a Charlie, a Cliff and me, Larry. Oh! There was also a Bob, who was a Federal Aviation Administrator (FAA) doctor in the course.

Ten residents and staff

Aerospace medicine differs from standard medical school training in that it addresses the physical and physiological changes to which a body is subjected and must tolerate under the stresses of flying, especially in a modern jet aircraft.

First we have to deal with the altitude and its two "troublemakers," low atmospheric pressure and (as a result) decreased oxygen availability to the lungs. To detail what I mean, let me explain it as follows:

> Air has weight and that weight presses on the body to the tune of about 14.7 pounds for every square inch of surface. This is at sea level where we are said to be experiencing one Atmosphere. Air has approximately 21% oxygen, but that 14.7 pounds psi is sufficient to ensure your blood, which carries the oxygen through your system, will be about 95% saturated—and that is normal. When we ascend to an altitude of ten thousand feet we lose about 4.5 pounds of that 14.7 pounds of pressure, but we can still manage with the resultant 90% oxygen saturation—if we are not doing too much strenuous work. The higher you go, the lower the pressure, and the less oxygen for your blood and your body. But the decreasing pressure goes down exponentially, not in a straight line, so that at only eighteen thousand feet, one is actually at only half an atmosphere, with 7.34 psi, and one cannot survive at that altitude without either supplemental oxygen or being pressurized, as we are on commercial airline flights. Most civilian airliners are pressurized to keep the passengers at the atmospheric equivalent of seven or eight thousand feet, even though the aircraft may be operating at about thirty-five thousand feet. Outside a pressurized aircraft at 35,000 feet, one would have to breathe 100% pure oxygen to stay conscious. Once you are over forty thousand feet, the atmosphere is so low that even 100% oxygen would not suffice, and additional pressure has to

> be used to force oxygen into the lungs. So, in a cabin not pressurized, one has to wear a pressure mask or, better yet, a pressure suit.

All this knowledge did very little to allay my concerns when they told me that part of my training program involved sitting in a vacuum chamber that would take me to the equivalent of seventy-five thousand feet. This meant I would be above 93% of the earth's atmosphere with only 1.03 psi on my body instead of the normal 14.7 pounds! I was also reminded that if unprotected at about sixty-three thousand feet one's blood begins to boil. Welcome to "Anxiety Theater." But, as I was told, it would be no problem.

I would be in the MC-4 Partial Pressure Suit. This fantastic piece of torture equipment would squeeze my whole body more and more as I progressed through altitudes over forty thousand feet and force 100% oxygen into my lungs to the point where inhalation was not really an option. My biggest problem would be exhaling! It took great effort to blow out against the pressurized oxygen that you inhaled.

Actually, an average human could probably do this for only two-to-three minutes before the muscles of the chest gave out. I don't know what caused Francis Gary Powers to descend in his U-2 over Russia many years ago, but at the altitude he was flying, he probably had two minutes (or less) to get that aircraft down below thirty-to-forty thousand feet before he would expire—that is, if his mechanical problem involved loss of pressurization.

I was assured my physiological parameters would be monitored from the outside of the chamber at all times as I was being observed through very thick glass portholes. I was wired with electrocardiograph leads and suited up. The chamber door was closed tightly, and the vacuum suction pumps went to work.

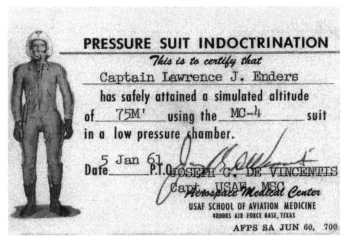

MC-4 training certificate

There were no problems at twenty five thousand feet. At nearly forty thousand feet, the pressure suit mechanism kicked in and began to squeeze my entire body. As I continued to climb, the pressure breathing began, and it was difficult to speak as oxygen was continually forced into my lungs. I could only mutter a few words with my labored exhalation.

After reaching sixty thousand feet, things turned downright uncomfortable. At this time communication was almost impossible, my heart rate was climbing, and my chest muscles were beginning to ache. At seventy thousand feet, I could hear the chamber operators contacting me, but could only respond by moving my head for a "yes" or a "no."

At seventy-five thousand feet, I was miserable and absolutely sure I would die if they didn't bring me down soon. There was a red button I could push if there was an emergency and if I began to lose consciousness. Of course, no "macho" trainee would ever do that! Even so, only the operators outside the chamber could bring me back down. After two minutes at that extreme altitude my cardiograph warning signal went off outside the chamber; I was consistently skipping heart beats and my heart rate was up to over 200 beats per minute.

I remember hearing a voice saying "Are you ready to come down, Doc?" I thought they would never ask! I gave one short nod of my head and I heard that chamber begin to hiss as beautiful, normal air began to come back in. We did a quick drop to fifty thousand feet and then a more gradual descent as the suit released its pressure on me. By the time I "hit the ground," so to speak, I was pretty well wrung-out and couldn't get out of that suit fast enough!

I soon learned that this was only the beginning of the "torture testing."

6

~ No Jumping, Please! ~

Next lesson: To exit a jet aircraft flying at three or four hundred miles an hour.

In an emergency, one cannot simply slide open the canopy, climb out, and then leap into the "wild blue" expecting your parachute to do the right thing. One must be technically "blown" out of the plane. Enter the Ejection Seat.

The ejection seat mechanism for the training program at that time was rigged so that once you positioned yourself in the seat with your feet back, back straight, and your head against the back rest, you'd raise the left arm rest which would blow off your canopy. Then you simply raised the right arm-rest and squeezed the trigger which would fire the seat, hopefully, with you and your parachute still in it.

Once out of the plane and free-falling in your seat, you needed to kick away from the seat and deploy your 'chute. Now in the more modern fighter aircrafts, firing handles have been relocated to make them more accessible. Once you are out of the aircraft, there is an automatic system which separates you from the seat and another which deploys the parachute for you. However, when I was going through the training, it was still pretty much "do it yourself."

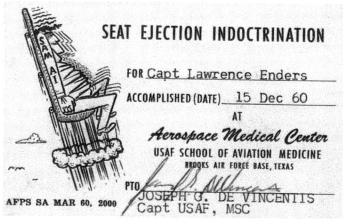

Ejection seat training certificate

Ejection training on the ground is accomplished by rigging an aircraft seat so that the back of it is attached to a forty-foot vertical rail. Imagine, if you will, that you have a forty-foot vertical ladder, and you've taken a kitchen chair and somehow attached the back of it to the ladder so it can slide up and down. The question is: What will propel that chair or in our case, the aircraft seat, up that vertical rail? Now the masterminds of the time concluded that a 20mm cannon shell under the seat would do the job. Of course it would! The training procedure was basically clear cut—strap yourself into the seat, make sure you are in the correct position with everything straight, left arm-rest "up," right arm-rest "up," squeeze the trigger and BAM! Off you go. Consequently, there were a lot of sore tailbones and backaches as rewards for doing a good job!

To get an unbiased critique of this system, take a shotgun shell, set it upright with the primer facing down, and find a mouse that is willing to sit on top of that shotgun shell while you fire it. Ask the mouse how he liked the ride (if you can find him).

Following a significant number of serious back injuries to fliers, the designers decided to make some changes by placing a small rocket under the seat. A rocket when fired begins somewhat slower and then builds up speed. Watch a space launch and you'll see it in slow motion. The new system has considerably reduced the incidence of back injury to ejecting pilots.

"*We found the aircraft carrier.*"

Cliff and Larry on board the carrier

Want to try doing something equally as scary? Participate in landing a plane on an aircraft carrier. A part of our academic program included a week's exchange with the Navy, and believe me, it made us appreciate those nice long concrete runways we have in the Air Force. At about twelve thousand feet a carrier looks not unlike a postage stamp. Unfortunately, as one flies lower, the size doesn't seem to change very much. But the pilots we were flying with managed to get us on the deck and keep us out of the ocean. Participating in carrier operations during a mock submarine attack was fantastic. So hats off to our sister service!

The altitude chamber is where you get to experience hypoxia, the shortage of oxygen. This was a snap compared to the MC-4 jaunt. To experience hypoxia we were required to pair off inside the altitude chamber. One of the partners wears his oxygen mask, and the other has his hanging loosely without covering his face. At about fourteen to fifteen thousand feet, the unmasked partner will begin to experience disorientation, blurred vision, and poor coordination. At this time the oxygen deprived trainee should have his oxygen mask replaced by his partner. We each had faith in our partner because his turn was next. If he let you pass out, revenge time is nearby!

I have always believed in the words of wisdom "if it ain't broke, don't fix it." So if an airplane still has a good engine and the wings are still on, don't jump out of it. But the Air Force, in their infinite wisdom, decreed that anyone who ventures into the sky must be prepared for all eventualities. That led to the next four of five "exercises" in the series, "How Else Can We Hurt These Guys?"

I suppose it makes sense that should you have to exit your aircraft in an emergency, you ought to know how to control your parachute and land properly without breaking every bone in your body.

It's called Jump School.

7

~ Oh, 'Chute! ~

They were kind enough not to push us out of an airplane. Jump towers would suffice. This would also save the Government money by not having to replace damaged physicians. The release towers weren't all that bad. You were harnessed into an open parachute, hoisted to the top of the tower by a cable, and when the top-most point of your 'chute hit the switch, it released you. The 'chute was already unfolded to its full length and would simply billow out as it filled with air during the drop.

The main purpose of this was to teach the trainee how to handle the risers which control the direction of travel of a parachute. The risers are the straps that connect your harness near the shoulder up to your parachute cords on either side; which, in turn, are attached to the nylon 'chute itself.

Our next objective is to land into the wind. This serves two purposes. One, it slows the forward motion of the jumper as he lands; two, when you do hit the ground, it tends to blow the collapsing 'chute back to your rear so it doesn't come down over your head. If one releases the 'chute attachment buckles as soon as one hits the ground, the 'chute won't drag you across the ground with it.

The more traumatic part of that training program was the low level jump platform. About eight feet high and no 'chute required, it was designed for the trainee to practice the landing. We learned how to bend our knees slightly and then use them as "shock absorbers." We also learned how to curl the body and do a roll so as to spread the impact forces caused by meeting the ground at speed. So you stand at the edge of the platform and jump, bend your knees, hit the ground, and do your roll. Sounds easy, right? Wrong! We had ten guys with very painful knees and backs and with multiple bruises before the class was over.

Flying over water can produce a completely different set of difficult situations, so it was off to Water Survival School. This was all handled in a very large lake in northern Texas. There we donned all the equipment that could either save your life or drown you. The outcome depended entirely upon the trainee exercising a precise, proper procedure in the correct order, and then executing the proper steps to utilize the equipment. Do it properly, you survive. Mess it up, you can drown.

Getting outfitted for this exercise reminds me a lot of one great scene in the movie, "The Graduate." At the college graduation party for the son, the father had the young man don a complete underwater ensemble—a full body wet suit, headgear, mask, snorkel tube, and spear gun. He was then coaxed into the family swimming pool so that all the neighbors could see this fantastic gift at work. Thinking back on that scene, it would have been far easier than our drill.

When a pilot has a mission that is likely to be over a huge tract of water, he is outfitted with additional survival equipment. Assuming a jet aircraft is to be used for the mission, the pilot begins with his own basic gear—flight suit, boots, and a hard helmet complete with an oxygen mask. He also wears a deflated life vest with bottled CO_2 to inflate the vest if needed. His back rest is his parachute. Beneath his "sit upon," instead of the normal seat pad, a very thin pad covers a water survival kit which is relatively large and heavy. The kit contains an inflatable one-man life raft and signaling devices such as a flashing beacon, a mirror, sometimes a locator transmitter; and in case you have the opportunity to extend your one-man cruise, some fishing gear.

If a pilot must eject, for example, at twenty-five thousand feet, he needs to remember that ALL the gear attached to his body is going with him. Again, there is a very precise sequence of events which the pilot must follow if he chooses not to drown. First, he separates from his ejection seat and then "free falls" for some distance. The newer systems will automatically deploy the parachute at a lower altitude where the pilot can breathe the more acceptably oxygenated air without a mask. The 'chute opening will give him a bit of a jolt since he is quite heavy due to the added weight. The oxygen mask was only providing proper air to the pilot when it was attached to the regulator inside the aircraft. Now, at a safe altitude he can release the mask so that it hangs down to the side.

You start controlling the direction of your 'chute but you cannot expect to stay afloat, or even handle the water landing, with all that equipment weighing you down. You need to open the two release catches for the survival kit and drop it away from your body. The kit is still attached to the pilot via a lanyard, otherwise it may well be out of reach of a downed pilot when he finally settles into the water. When the survival gear reaches the end of the length of lanyard, some twenty five feet, it automatically deploys and inflates the life raft. The pilot will then be able to pull the raft and its contents to him after he finally splashes down.

By the time he does all this, he will be very close to the water. At this point he needs to inflate his personal life vest by pulling on the two inflation cords. Now comes a pilot's judgment call based on how well he absorbed his training. Both hands must go up to the two parachute riser releases, each of which has a safety cover. The "trick" is to remove the safety covers and then operate the release buckles just as he hits the water. The ideal time is the moment the toes of his boots break water. Three or four seconds later he could be in the water, struggling to stay afloat with his 'chute still attached. The 'chute will either try to pull him through the water, if there is any wind, or collapse all around his head.

Both scenarios have the potential to drown the pilot. On the other hand, if his judgment is off and he releases the 'chute buckles before he hits the water, he's going to free fall with all his gear and that is definitely *not* good. When descending rapidly, judging distance to the water is very difficult. I'd love to meet the guy who can tell me with complete accuracy when he is just a foot or two above the water so he can release his 'chute "by the book." Even executing all the procedures exactly "by the book," the unexpected can always happen. On a very calm day, even assuming you released all your gear and the 'chute (just as you touch the water), if the 'chute is still fully deployed, it could still settle gently right over your head.

If this happens, we were instructed "not to panic!" Your life vest will keep you afloat even under the wet nylon canopy. Struggling wildly with the canopy over your head could quite easily cause you to become completely tangled in the cords and the nylon cloth. People have drowned in this situation.

A parachute canopy is configured much like an umbrella canopy. On an umbrella all the support struts meet at a point at the top. On a parachute those "support struts" are the sewn seams joining the nylon panels. By simply finding a seam and gently pulling yourself along it, you'll eventually come to the edge of the canopy and out into the open. Then you can pull your raft to you, via the lanyard, slide aboard, and wait to be rescued.

If you are asking how you train for all of these contingencies without actually being up in the air, the answer is "para-sailing."

On a small island in that same lake in Texas, the trainee, fully equipped with all the gear described above and attached to a large para-sail, stands on the beach facing into the wind. A powerful speedboat with a very long nylon cord attached to the trainee's waist waits for the word while two sturdy "helpers" hold the canopy edges of the open para-sail so the wind can balloon it out. At a signal, the power boat speeds off, dunks the trainee into the water and then, with any luck, he is hoisted into the air. At several hundred feet and at a signal from the boat, the trainee releases the tow line and begins his descent. From about three hundred feet, the trainee has approximately thirty seconds to execute all the procedures in sequence before hitting the water. Once proficient in all aspects of water survival, one just hoped it would never be needed in a real life situation.

8

~ This Is Surviving? ~

The Survival School Training Program came in a series. Water Training was followed by Arctic Survival, Jungle Survival, and, finally, Mountain Survival. The Arctic Training in Alaska was aimed mainly at how to get out of the cold, build an igloo, start a small fire with canned fuel, and eat *pemmican bars*. These bars consisted of lard impregnated with a few specks of ground beef. Talk about gourmet!

Jungle Survival took place down in Panama. If one had to eject over a jungle, you'd hopefully end up on the ground with your parachute, a survival knife, and whatever else you had in your pockets. Our instructors took us, three at a time, far up a jungle river in a small boat. With deployed parachutes wadded up under one arm, we were then "dumped" in about three feet of water to make our way to the river bank on our own. We did have waterproof matches with us, which we carried in our flight suits. Best of all, we had a map of the area. Our objective was to find our way back to the training camp which was located about five miles away through the jungle. Our instructors, being the good fellows that they were and not wanting us to go hungry on our little adventure, gave each of us the tail of a decent sized iguana—raw, of course!

Each of us also had three small tins of hard candy and a little bit of cheese. I think I heard, "Bon appetite," as the boat pulled away from us, but I can't be sure. During the lecture portion of our training for this fun trip, we had been shown how to make a hammock from our parachutes. With the ample supply of parachute cord available, finding two stout trees about eight or ten feet apart really wasn't a problem. Staying in a hammock all night, let alone sleeping in one, now *that* was a problem! Almost impossible.

In the jungle at night, dark is really dark, and we could hear all the critters out there, scrambling through the undergrowth as well as through the trees. With snakes and insects in abundance, the idea of sleeping on the ground was dismissed immediately.

Finding dry wood for a fire was also a problem. We found that a few older, somewhat dried out vines, worked best and we drew straws to determine who would be the cook. I escaped that chore. Dinner preparation was pretty simple. Skin the iguana tail, poke a sharp stick through the length of it, and hold it over a small fire. We learned two things from the exercise. First, make sure the stick is very green or it will burn through before the meat is cooked. Second, our cook could forget any dreams he may have had of becoming a Master Chef!

Obviously, our instructors were a lot smarter than we were. One of us had taken some packets of salt and pepper from the mess hall the day before and carried them in his flight suit pocket. His intention was to add some flavor to improve the taste of our next "surprise" meal. However, after we were dumped in three feet of water, the condiments were completely useless. I guess our instructors were used to such attempts to make the lizard tail tasty! But, as with all strange meat being cooked over a small fire in the great outdoors and being eaten for the first time, it tasted just like chicken. *Forgive me. That was a lie!* It tasted like you would expect the tail of an iguana to taste!

And what was there to drink with this appetizing meal? River water, of course. We filled our small canteens and dropped in a few iodine tablets, which the Air Force issued, designed to kill pathogens (bad germs) in suspect water. You must wait for several hours before drinking the water so that the little pills can do their work. The iodine may have rendered the germs harmless, but it didn't really lend much to the taste.

Bedtime was when the daylight ended at around nine o'clock. This was followed by about eight hours of non-sleep . . . trying not to fall out of our hammocks, listening to all the noises around and above us, and hoping the slithering noises from below stayed below!

Early next morning, after a breakfast of one hard piece of candy and one piece of cheese, we studied the map and saw that the river curved a lot but eventually came fairly close to our destination. It seemed logical that we should follow the river bank. That turned out to be the right thing to do—but not the easiest. Actually, the hardest part was having to cut our way through the dense thicket which tore at our nylon flight suits and scratched our arms, legs, and any other exposed skin that came in contact with the myriad of sharp bits of jungle foliage.

Our parachutes were rather bulky so rolling them up and carrying them was not easy. We stopped on our trek at one clear spot we found and decided to work smarter. Cutting off some of the nylon cords, we configured the 'chutes into quite small rolls, tied them with the cords, and then slung them like knapsacks on our backs. Any item of any use would be rolled into the 'chute to carry. It also occurred to us that tying one of our survival knives to a stout stick gave us a spear. Though I am not quite sure what we intended to do with it.

But we were actually starting to use our heads which, of course, was the lesson we were supposed to learn from this course. The trek back to the base was accomplished in about two-and-a-half days. It wasn't really all that far, and the goal of the course was not just to force us to walk through the jungle for days. The bottom line was to teach us to think under adverse conditions, to improvise, and use our heads to overcome all the problems we were likely to encounter.

On the morning we were to fly out of Panama and back to Texas, one of our instructors, a sergeant, showed us his personal "enterprise." His hobby was to take large, old, sturdy saw blades, grind them down to machete size, sharpen them, and equip them with wooden grips. He'd then sell the piece for ten dollars. I can assure you, each of us would have liked to have one of them during our trek through that Panamanian jungle! I'm not sure why, but all ten of us arrived in Texas with a nice, shiny machete wrapped in underwear in our flight bags. For the Texas jungle, of course!

9

~ This Is The Pits! ~

All this was going on during what was referred to as the Cold War with Russia in the early sixties. If a flier was operating near a foreign border, there was always a chance he could go down in their territory. The final survival course was designed to expose us to two situations. The first was Escape and Evasion. Assuming you reached the ground alive, you needed to hide until either rescue arrived or you found your own way back to friendly territory. In the meantime, you had to assume that the enemy was out there looking for you.

The second situation, and a much less comfortable one, was to give students a taste of what it would be like if they were to be captured, held prisoner, and interrogated. There is a small military base deep in the foothills of the eastern slopes of the Cascade Mountains in Washington State. Manned by "aggressor" soldiers, it is an "enemy" base for these exercises. They wear black and gray uniforms, unlike any of the other US Forces. The job of the designated Aggressor Forces is to find you, capture you, incarcerate you, and interrogate you. This is done sometimes by means that are, shall we say, less than comfortable in order to extract any pertinent military information you may have.

Of course, these are all American soldiers acting as aggressors, but they do what must be done to accomplish their mission. Obviously, they are not permitted to do "significant" bodily harm to their prisoners (after all, we were all on the same side), but "significant" may well be relative. The men of the aggressor forces were carefully selected. The task of being "the bad guy" and treating you harshly may well be satisfying to some people.

As a result, all volunteers for the aggressor force were subjected to detailed psychiatric and psychological evaluations. Those with passive aggressive and/or hostile tendencies are weeded out. Even so, I have been told that an aggressor or two have had to be dismissed from the "enemy" force because it was noted they were liking the job a little too much and seemed to forget that it was merely a training course and that their "captives" were really fellow Americans.

This Survival Course was saved for last. The ten of us were flown out in a C-131 to Fairchild Air Force Base, Washington State. We boarded a military truck and were driven for a few hours through the forest and the foothills to a facility occupied by the "enemy." We were taken directly to an area that was different from any other base we'd seen thus far. There was a small mess hall and a dormitory with twelve beds and lockers for our gear. Outside, in front of the quarters, was a small amphitheater that had a wired sound system and a podium set up for an instructor. Two days were spent on presentations about survival, escape, and evasion in a hostile environment.

The third day was "evasion day." Let me give you a scenario of what this exercise involved:

First, we would have parachuted down into enemy territory. While trying to reach a rendezvous point, we needed to remain undetected by the enemy unit which was searching for us. Flight suits, parachutes, and survival knives were a part of our gear. Next, we were taken about four miles into the mountains and shown on a map where our home base was located.

Heading out for escape and evasion training

At a certain hour a flare was fired and that meant that the "enemy" was looking for us. There were mountain streams where we could use our parachutes to seine for small fish. Obviously, any fire had to be small and smokeless or the enemy would pinpoint our location very quickly. We walked quietly and carefully, and only once did we see our pursuers. That night we wrapped ourselves in our 'chutes and slept under brush. Looking back, I don't think they were trying very hard to find us. I believe that the exercise was more tuned to having us out there in unfamiliar territory and having to use our heads to remain undetected.

The exercise ended at dark the second night; we had a good meal and were advised to get to bed early. Very early, at about one o'clock in the morning, a training team came into our dormitory and rousted us out of our beds, instructing us to don coveralls which they had brought with them. We were not permitted to wear any of our own clothing or to have on our bodies any article of a personal nature.

The reason soon became obvious to us. They herded us into the back of a truck and we were taken to a field about the dimensions of a professional football field. It certainly wasn't there for football, though. This field had trenches, each about four feet deep, furrowed across it about every fifteen yards. And the surface of the field was not smooth but had rocks, tree stumps, and small hillocks scattered about. Of course, at that time of the morning, it was still dark and we could not see the other end of the field, but we assumed that it was the same. The hillocks seemed to be about three or four feet high. There were two small lights at our end of the field which allowed us to gain an impression of what lay before us.

We discovered that the field was covered with a grid of barbed wire, a bit like a "king sized" screen, about three to four feet above the ground as far as the eye could see. The opening squares between the wires were no more than two feet by two feet. The scenario was this: *We were downed pilots attempting to evade and escape from the enemy.*

We had to crawl under the barbed wire grid the entire length of the field. The enemy, knowing we were in the area, would be searching for us. We could hide in the trenches, but that was not a good idea, or take cover behind or beside all the many natural obstacles on the field. The enemy would patrol around the outside edges of the field and, every now and then, from a fixed bunker, a burst of machine gun fire would erupt just to make sure we remembered to keep our heads down. Periodically, a flare would be launched to facilitate our discovery. All of these were guaranteed to deter you from getting to your feet and stretching your aching limbs. Our pursuers also had guns and flashlights. Of course, there was a "carrot" for us. We had been told that anyone who made it the length of the field without being captured by the enemy would receive a pass to the mess hall the next night for a big steak dinner with all the trimmings.

They started us two at a time at five-minute intervals with a fifteen-yard lateral separation into the first trench, and then they left us on our own. Fifteen or twenty feet ahead of us was total darkness. Fortunately, the sky was clear and a little night vision kicked in. Of course, it was belly work all the way. We slithered our way out of one trench into the next, around a hillock, behind a tree stump or a rock, always hugging Mother Earth. Every now and then we'd see a flashlight and have to remain still and hidden. Then there would be a burst of machine gun fire across our route, just to keep it interesting.

And interesting it was, with more experiences ahead of us. Just minutes after we started, I lost touch with my "wing man," not that I was trying to stay near him as everyone was really on his own. Nevertheless, we lost contact. As I continued to slither on the ground with my already scraped knees and elbows covered with dirt, I occasionally would get my posterior coveralls snagged by barbed wire. That was not pleasant!

After about half an hour, I noticed that the gunfire had lessened, as had the flares, and I saw fewer flashlight beams. I was actually starting to believe that I might make it. It must have been around three or three thirty in the morning when I thought I could see a tree line silhouetted in the distance. Shortly after, I was sure they were trees and that meant that I must be nearing the end of the field . . . getting a lot closer to that promised steak dinner. The course did, indeed, stop right at the tree line.

I saw and heard no one and began to climb slowly out of the trench, sensing victory, face down on the "free ground." All right!! I was one happy Fly Boy—right up to the point where I felt the rifle barrel touching the back of my neck and a broken voice saying, "You are my prisoner." My hands were bound behind my back, and I was marched through a copse of trees to a parking area and loaded into the back of a canvas-covered truck. To my surprise, five of my compatriots were already in there, being held captive, and in the next thirty or so minutes the rest of our group joined us. I couldn't believe that none of us had managed to evade the enemy. Later it was explained to us that nobody was actually searching for us. Those soldiers around the edge were just flashing lights and making noise so that we would concentrate on the task at hand. But the main group of enemy soldiers were hidden in the tree line, just waiting patiently for us to step out of the last trench into their rifles. We were all dead ducks from the very start. If not, how could we be assured of experiencing what was to come next?

It was just about dawn when our trucks pulled up to the prison camp. The compound was some two-hundred-and-fifty feet square and surrounded by a fence of barbed wire, ten feet tall interlaced with, and topped with, razor wire. There were four guard towers, one at each corner of the compound, manned at all times by soldiers armed with machine guns. There were also two or three small buildings over on one side of the camp.

Guards patrolled the perimeter just outside the fence, and we saw a few of the aggressor forces personnel going in and out of the buildings. The chains on the gate were unlocked to allow us to be hauled inside, then quickly locked again. Only then did we notice a number of corrugated metal roofing panels, about six feet by ten, lying flat on the ground. There were three rows of four with about ten feet between adjacent panels. We were lined up and searched, even though we had already been searched when first captured.

Four members of the aggressor forces went to the first panel, one at each corner. They lifted the panel to reveal a hole in the ground, measuring approximately five feet wide by nine feet long, and about five feet deep. Apart from a wooden bucket in one corner, there was nothing else in the hole. A couple of the guards took two of the prisoners, untied their hands, and pushed them towards the first pit. We all got the idea very quickly that this was to be our accommodations, two to a pit. The dimensions of our new "lodgings" were quite deliberate. One could lay down on the dirt floor but no one could stand upright. Because of the corrugated metal roof only a bit of daylight slipped in between the metal and the ground. But at night very little of the lighting around the fence was able to penetrate.

The bucket was, of course, our toilet facility—so much for privacy. That was a luxury prisoners could not afford. We had nothing to eat that morning. Our "exercise" was limited to a half hour in the morning and again in the afternoon, just a walk around in the compound and always under the sharp scrutiny of the guards. That was the only time we all saw each other.

During our training leading up to this situation, it had been burned into our memory that we give our captors nothing more than our name, rank and serial number . . . and always be on the lookout for a way to escape. However, flat ground, high fences and lots of guards gave us the feeling that escape was not likely. Perhaps we may have had an opportunity to escape if we were taken outside the fence, but that did not happen.

That afternoon, after we were allowed to clean out our buckets, we were given some water and two pieces of dry bread. Most of the time we sat on the ground in the hole and talked about escape but, sadly, none of us were able to come up with any feasible plan. About nine o'clock that evening, we were given a little broth and a few carrots for dinner. We had no idea what the origin of the broth may have been (and probably didn't want to know).

That night the loudspeakers in the compound announced, about every hour, that anyone attempting to escape would be shot. Sleep was difficult, at best. The next morning we were all very hungry, indeed; and it seemed a lot more than forty hours since we had our last decent meal. And to our surprise, we were told that we would actually have a hot breakfast. We could even smell the coffee brewing!

We were taken out one at a time and escorted to the cooking area behind one of the small wooden buildings. I was told that they had boiled some potatoes and cabbage and had made fresh coffee. Not exactly a great breakfast menu. But we were going to be given a choice—potatoes or cabbage or coffee. Or, if we chose, we could have all three. For a dish, I was given a one pound coffee tin, empty and sans top.

One by one, at about three-minute intervals, we were marched behind one of the buildings where a long, roughly hewn table held three large pots.

Behind each of the pots, stood one of the aggressor forces soldiers. One asked, "You want all three?" Of course I wanted all three—I was *hungry*. So the first man took my dish and spooned in a few pieces of over-done, mushy potato which fell apart as soon as it hit bottom. He then handed the dish to the next server who added a few leaves of cooked cabbage. The last person to serve me was standing over a very dark brew of strong coffee . . . and laughing. You guessed it. He took a ladle of the coffee, grounds included, and poured it directly over the mushy potatoes and cabbage. I don't know about the expression on my face at that time, but they sure seemed to think it was all very funny. *I didn't.*

Evidently this was picnic day because I was led to a log where I could sit and enjoy my "feast." I looked into my can and saw bits of cabbage leaves floating in the coffee, including the grounds from the bottom of the kettle, and the potato disintegrating in the whole mess. I was almost tempted to dump it out but my empty stomach got the better of me and I managed to down it all, including the floating coffee grounds. If you are cooking and like to create unusual concoctions, try it sometime . . . but it's not recommended if you are expecting guests.

About noon the other member of my "pit" was taken away, and he never returned. At about three o'clock in the afternoon, they came for me. Again, my hands were tied behind my back and I was marched out through the gate under double guard. They had placed a rope around my neck and one of them led me like a dog on a leash. They took me along a path to another small building amongst the trees.

The sign above the door read "Interrogation Facility." The inside of the one-room shack was very sparsely outfitted with one desk, one chair, one interrogator, and one three-foot length of broom handle. The only light came from a single bulb dangling on a cord below a ceiling beam. The interrogation began.

> "Are you Captain Enders?"
> "Yes."
> "What is your Unit?"
> "Captain Enders, 76428."
> "I asked what unit you belong to. What were you doing in our air space?"
> "Captain Lawrence Enders, 76428."

This went on for several minutes before he let me know that if I didn't give him the information he wanted, my life would become very uncomfortable. I did what I was supposed to and gave him nothing more than my name, rank, and serial number. This seemed to cause him some exasperation. After another moment he said to me, "Take off your clothes. All of them." I said, "You're kidding." He replied, "You can do it or we will do it . . . your choice."

I stripped them off and stood before him, totally naked. He ordered me to kneel down, under the one light bulb, and he began to examine me closely, all the time making every kind of comment imaginable in order to humiliate me. Then the questioning started again. The same questions from him, the same answers from me. After another ten minutes, the two guards were called in. My hands were untied and, while still on my knees, he had me clasp my hands behind my head and lean back as far as I could. There were no questions at that time. After just a short time in that position, my back began to ache and I started to straighten up to ease the pain.

He said to the two guards, "I see this man needs some help." They let me kneel up straight for a moment while one of the guards got the broom handle and laid it across the back of my legs, just behind my knees. Then they pushed me back into the "lean back" position. It didn't take long for the broom handle to produce significant pain and cut off the circulation to my legs. In about ten minutes, my legs were numb from the knees down and the pain got worse. Shortly after that I fell over. They picked me up, let me straighten for a minute, and then put me back in the same position, complete with broom handle behind my knees. It is an extremely painful position and I recommend that you "do not try this at home." After several minutes, I really thought I was going to pass out.

They were watching me carefully. Then to my surprise the interrogator stood up, removed the broom handle, and helped me dress. It took some minutes for the circulation to come back to my legs during which time the interrogator congratulated me on completing the course. I was tempted to call him a few choice names, but this was a training course, wasn't it? Although I didn't get my steak dinner, there was good food waiting for me just a few hundred yards away.

There was a debriefing the next morning before our departure from this particular slice of paradise. To all, it was made quite clear that the "minor discomfort" which we had experienced the day before was a walk in the park—a piece of cake—compared to what we could expect if we were really captured in enemy territory. After talking with some of the Vietnam prisoners, I knew the interrogator was telling the truth.

10

~ The Gravity Of It All ~

When we returned to the School of Aerospace Medicine, we found that our next topic for discussion was Gravity. For instance, when you are just sitting quietly in your chair, you are experiencing a downwards force of +1G, which is the name given to the Earth's gravitational pull on a stationary object.

We were now going to be introduced to too much gravity and then too little or Zero gravity. There is really no limit to the speed one can endure in straight and level movement, for instance in flight. But change the direction (or the speed) and the G forces come into play. Imagine, if you will, that you put your aircraft into a steep dive at around four hundred mph and you pull out of that dive. Suddenly, the weight of the gravitational force doubles, triples or even quadruples, pulling down on your body, all depending on the sharpness of the pull-out at the end of the dive.

You may have experienced some of these same effects on a roller coaster or a Tilt-A-Whirl. Your sitting position makes all the difference in the world. Rapid acceleration has the same effect. Have you noticed, watching some space flight launches, that the crew members are laying on their backs in the capsule before lift off? The rocket accelerates upwards and they are subjected to G-forces, mainly from the front of them, pushing toward their backs. Drag racing will produce the same effect when accelerating, as are the pilots being catapulted off an aircraft carrier. You do pretty well in that configuration, but G-forces from head to foot are not tolerated very well. Our heart needs to pump blood to our head to keep the brain oxygenated, and the head-to-foot G-force counteracts that blood flow. The result can be unconsciousness.

At the Aerospace Medical Center, we had a great human centrifuge. By repositioning the seat inside the capsule on the centrifuge, on the end of a long arm, the capsule is spun around at any chosen speed and we can create any level of G-forces we wish from any direction. We all found out what our tolerances were. Actually, what was more exciting was to experience Zero Gravity, even though it lasted for only forty-five or fifty seconds at a time. While positive G-forces are relatively easy to produce on the human centrifuge, Zero G is a little more difficult and cannot be simulated on the ground.

A specially-designed, large aircraft having a good sized cargo or passenger area, is completely gutted down to its bare bulkheads. Then it is heavily padded with a thick, quilt-like material. The aircraft engines are fitted with a force-feed fuel system in lieu of the gravity fuel feed systems normally used in a propeller driven aircraft.

The "zero gravity" aircraft

The subjects, in this instance being the ten of us, sit on the floor of the "padded cell" while the crew takes the plane to a high altitude. They dive the plane to increase the speed, then pull out of the dive into a steep climb. When the plane reaches the peak of its climb, just at the limit of its power and just prior to a stall, the nose is pushed over and the throttles are pulled back. The plane is then in "free fall" as is everybody in it, resulting in a relative Zero G situation for the passengers. For about forty-five to fifty seconds, the students float freely in the cabin, bouncing off the walls, doing somersaults or just wallowing!

Imagine yourself in an elevator on the 100th floor of a very tall building. All of a sudden the support cable breaks! Both you and the elevator are falling at the same speed so you are relatively "weightless" inside that box. Of course the stop at the end is quite dramatic and not recommended. Unfortunately, when the pilot pushes the throttles on and brings the plane out of its free fall, we immediately go from Zero G to about two or three +G's for several seconds. The whole maneuver can be repeated as long as there is fuel—or until too many students lose their stomach contents.

This is how the first astronauts became acquainted with Zero G.

In addition to our classroom sessions at SAM (School of Aerospace Medicine), we had frequent trips to other technological or academic institutions for short courses in special areas. At Kirkland AFB in New Mexico, we learned more about the physiological effects of radiation from whatever source of exposure. At the Center for Disease Control in Atlanta, Georgia, we became well-versed in National and International infectious diseases and their epidemiology. We had all been vaccinated for worldwide duty. That meant not only getting the vaccines for Tetanus, Typhus and Measles but also for Cholera, Polio, Smallpox, Plague and other diseases to which we might be exposed. At Fort Dietrich, Maryland, we studied chemical and biological warfare consequences. At MIT there was a two-week course in the physiological changes in the spectrum of Undersea and Aerospace Medicine.

The best short course we had was at Walter Reed Medical Center, near Washington DC. There we spent almost a week on the details of infectious diseases around the world and the currently available preventative measures we could use against them. The final session there was presented by a speaker whose name was Dr. John Enders. It was a very engrossing and thorough presentation, mostly on viral diseases. At the end of the talk I approached the speaker's rostrum because I wanted to tell him I had the same last name, and in fact my second name was John. I asked if he could spare a few minutes and he was gracious enough to do so.

It turned out that our ancestors, his and mine, all came to the United States from Germany. But that was not too surprising. I explained that while I was not much of a genealogist, my sister's son was quite interested in it, and he and his wife, after collecting all the information they could about the Enders side of the family in the States, traveled to Germany and began tracking them down. They ended up staying with an Enders family in a little town called Cobbenrode. The trail got pretty murky from there and they could not make any more progress. Dr. Enders could only remember that some of his relatives had mentioned living near Dortmund. A map showed that Cobbenrode is only fifteen miles southeast of Dortmund. We agreed we could be distant relatives and since he was about thirty years older than Me, maybe he was a long lost uncle. We settled for that and I was quite happy to "quit while I was ahead" in the genealogical hunt.

Why would I want to go further? My "maybe" uncle, and speaker for that day, was (it turned out) Dr. John Enders, winner of the **Nobel Prize in Physiology and Medicine** in 1954. He was the first man to culture the polio virus and attenuate it so that men like Jonas Salk and Dr. Saban could make the vaccines now used around the world. Of additional interest was that he had been a pilot in the Army Air Corps in 1918. I'll settle for an uncle like that anytime (even if it's only "maybe")!

The academic year ended at last, and we all went to our designated preceptor's locations for the final residency year. My preceptorship was relatively uneventful. In a Command Surgeon's office at Wright-Patterson AFB in Ohio I reviewed paperwork that needed to be concurred with at that level, participated in Command hospital inspections, and wrote a few papers. I guess it could be considered a one-year course in "how to be an administrator."

There was also considerable time to prepare for my board exams which would determine if I was actually qualified to be a Specialist in Aerospace Medicine certified by the American Board of Preventive Medicine. The testing consisted of two days of written exams and one day (actually three hours) of oral exams. Without keeping you in suspense, I actually did manage to pass the exams and, in fact, have a large, framed certificate on my office wall which proclaims my Specialty confirmation.

The last item of business ending the residency program was the selection and our notification of our new individual active duty assignments. I don't know who chose these locations (air bases) for us, but sometimes governmental decisions make one wonder. Budgets are always a problem and "holding down expenses" was the 11th Commandment. Eight of us were to be distributed all over the US, and two of us were posted overseas. In their infinite wisdom they assigned our only bachelor to Otis Air Force Base, Massachusetts, but assigned me, my wife, and five children to England! Talk about moving costs!

Our only bachelor was one of the Jim's, and he was a bit upset. Wouldn't England be a logical choice for a bachelor, and a stateside assignment be reasonable for a large family? Jim and I were both in agreement about this and presented that bit of logic to the powers that be for their pondering. For once they concurred with common sense. Jim happily went to England and my family and I trundled off to Otis Air Force Base, Massachusetts.

Serendipity stepped in again—positively for me—but very negatively for Jim.

Very early in Jim's assignment, I'm told on his third flight, Jim was killed. Would I have been in that aircraft had we not changed places? I have no idea, but I couldn't shake a slight feeling of guilt after encouraging our assignment swap.

11

~ A-Wackies & Bubbles ~

Otis AFB is on Cape Cod, Massachusetts, and its location alone set up a series of events that reflected very positively on my annual OER (Officers Efficiency Report). None of these things would have happened had I been assigned to any other base. The key ingredients in these serendipitous events at Otis were the immediate proximity of the Kennedy compound (as in John F. Kennedy, President of the United States), the Air Defense Command's Texas Towers out on the continental shelf, and the Atlantic Ocean itself. My assignment was as Chief Flight Surgeon for the Base. There were four flight Surgeons in total. My duties implicated me in the care of three separate functional units. The first, and largest, were the two squadrons of C-121 radar surveillance aircraft.

The EC-121 surveillance aircraft

In the "civilian world," this aircraft (built by Lockheed) was called the "Constellation." It was originally designed for commercial long overseas flights and was used widely by Pan Am. It flew with four powerful reciprocating engines and could stay aloft for more than twelve hours. The Air Force modified them, filled them with electronic gear and installed a big radar dome on top of the fuselage.

We are talking about the early sixties now, and the threat of war prompted the US to keep a sharp eye towards the Arctic area in the event foreign aircraft tried to enter our air space via the Polar route. Called AWACS, for Airborne Early Warning and Control System, the C-121's were programmed to fly a twelve hour racetrack course, up and down the northeast coast of the United States, scanning for enemy planes. The north bound leg of the track swung back towards the south at Newfoundland. The southbound track turned back to the north about a hundred miles north of Bermuda. Out west at McClellen Air Force Base, California, a sister organization of C-121's covered the northwest coast of the US. Directly north of the U.S. there were large land radar facilities spread across northern Canada, called the DEW (Distant Early Warning) line.

There was heavy use of all the C-121's and, with an aging fleet, it was not uncommon for at least one of the four engines to go out during a mission. The plane actually flew quite well on three engines, but safety regulations required that any malfunction of an engine was sufficient cause to abort the mission and for the plane to return to the nearest base for repairs.

As a result of those situations we would quite often not complete all twelve hours of flying. The smart pilots, even though we would lose an engine on the northbound track, would not declare the emergency until we had reached a point more than halfway down the south bound track.

Then, in the name of "safety," we would be "forced" to divert into Bermuda. There we'd have to sit it out and wait for parts to be flown in so the engine could be repaired. The crew would usually have to spend at least a day or two before the plane was, once again, sky-worthy. Interesting how many cases of Mateus Rosé (at only $2.50 per bottle), kidskin gloves, and purses managed to come back on board these flights. But then there has to be some compensation for mostly twelve hours of *complete boredom*!

The second unit I cared for at Otis was a small, but very lethal, ground-to-air-missile unit. For me, the most worrisome part of that unit was not the warheads but some of the major components of the propellant used to launch the missile. One of these components was UDMH (Unsymmetrical Di-Methyl Hydrazine). This was combined with an oxidizer, FRFNA (Red Fuming Nitric Acid). These chemicals can be stored in a rocket for quite some time, but there were always those days when the missile fuel would have to be downloaded and replaced with fresh fuel. Everyone held their breath on refueling days—literally. UDMH is very toxic and easily absorbed through the skin. The chemical is a known carcinogen. Of immediate danger was the fact that it can explode easily if any oxidizer is present. Needless to say, all medical personnel were on standby on refueling days.

The third unit, and one which received a great deal of my attention, was the "Texas Towers." There were times when weather conditions precluded the flights of the C-121's. Also, it was almost impossible for aircraft to be flying twenty four hours a day for three hundred and sixty-five days a year! To give our north east coast line constant coverage, at least from ground level (actually sea level), Air Defense Command had years earlier planned to build and install five Texas Towers in the Atlantic Ocean, numbered 1, 2, 3, 4, and 5. These were to extend from just east of Portland, Maine, to just off the lower coast of New Jersey.

Texas Tower #2

Texas Towers were very large platforms, so named because of the resemblance to oil-drilling platforms in the Gulf of Mexico. But these high, Air Force platforms were built to serve as radar sites. Only three... TT2, TT3 and TT4... were ever completed. The crews on each tower consisted of six officers and 48 men. TT2 and TT3 were located near the edge of the continental shelf in 56 and 80 feet of water, respectively. TT4, built in 1957, was anchored in 185 feet of water and needed added support of its three legs to compensate for the extra stresses of the sea's movement in water that deep. It never had the stability that had been expected. In 1958 and 1959, the Navy did some underwater structural work to try to strengthen the three supports of TT4.

But four powerful storms in 1959 and 1960 significantly affected the tower's stability and more braces were applied to the legs in 1960. On September 12, 1960, Hurricane Donna raged through the Tower area with winds reaching 132 mph, causing waves in excess of fifty feet and doing major damage to both the tower itself and its underpinnings. Extensive rebuilding of the under structure was scheduled for Spring of 1961, but before any major improvements were completed, another storm on January 14 and 15 with 35 foot waves and winds of 35 mph, snapped off one of the legs. At about 7:30 p.m. on January 25, Tower #4 collapsed with 28 men on board and sank to the bottom of the sea.

Following complete structural re-examination, it was determined that TT2 and TT3, having been built in relatively shallower water, need not be shut down. But some procedures had to be implemented to ensure the crews could be evacuated safely prior to any severe storm. There was, however, a major fly in that ointment. On several occasions, Russian trawlers were seen very close to the towers. As they were in International waters, there was nothing we could do to prevent their presence. If all crew members were to leave the tower, then under International Maritime Law an abandoned structure could be boarded by anyone and claimed as their own on the grounds of "salvage rights."

It was evident that some "stand by" crew would have to remain on board to prevent such action. Urgency was evident when a succession of storms struck TT2 and TT3 between October 1961 and March 1962, prompting evacuation of the regular crews ten times. Several experimental methods were considered and discarded. One viable option seemed to have merit, and it eventually became known as the Texas Tower Survival Capsule. It was a large, watertight, metal, ball-shaped capsule capable of holding seven men inside. It was equipped with enough food, water, and oxygen to sustain them underwater for fifteen days.

The Electric Boat Division of General Dynamics was selected to build it in New London, Connecticut.

The scenario would go something like this:

> *If a storm produced seas with 35-foot waves accompanied by winds of more then 50 mph, all regular crew members would be evacuated by helicopter or ship. The remaining seven men would stay with the tower. If the tower began to disintegrate and heavy seas and strong winds would preclude any further rescue attempts, the seven men would seal themselves inside the capsule and go down with the tower.*

> *The large sphere was attached to a huge block of concrete which would facilitate the sinking of the hollow ball. The men would ride out the storm on the ocean floor until it subsided. They would then release a radio antenna buoy which would allow them to contact US Navy surface ships standing by. After contact, the ships would pinpoint the location of the capsule and clear the surface above it to give the capsule an open area in which to ascend. At an agreed-upon time and count-down, the crew, strapped into their seats, would pull a lever which released the sphere from its concrete anchor. The capsule would then "pop" to the surface and the tower crew would be rescued.*

Texas Tower survival capsule readied for underwater testing

Capsule pops out of water when released

Construction of the survival capsule began shortly before I arrived at Otis. Soon thereafter, I was notified that I would be the "medical man" on site when the capsule was to be tested underwater, both unmanned and manned. It struck me then that I needed to be a bit more conversant with undersea medicine. I contacted Captain George Bond, the Commander of the US Naval Medical Research Laboratory located at the Submarine Base at New London, Connecticut, and requested a personal, quick, but more detailed course in "Submarine Medicine" at his facility. After explaining the whole Texas Towers situation and what I believed was my need for his tutoring, he agreed to see me, and off I went to the sub base. I had no idea that my mentor was a *legend* in the field of Underwater Medicine. After learning more about Captain Bond before heading his way, it was with great humility that I shook his hand upon my arrival.

Undersea Medicine is, in many ways, quite similar to Aerospace Medicine but physiologically at the exact opposite end of the spectrum. If a pilot goes up to altitude too fast and unprotected, he may get the "bends." Because air is mostly composed of nitrogen, we have a significant amount of that gas compressed in our body fluids under the one atmosphere in which we normally live. Rising out of and above the 14.7 psi too quickly can release the dissolved nitrogen, producing very painful bubbles in the joints and organs. In the spinal fluid, the wrong bubble in the wrong place can produce paralysis. These released bubble maladies are called the "bends."

In Submarine Medicine, a similar phenomenon can occur if a diver surfaces too fast. The deeper one goes and the longer one stays underwater, the more nitrogen is diffused into the body tissue and blood, so the ascent must be slower. To complicate it even more, at sea level we are at one atmosphere and we would need to climb hundreds of thousands of feet into the air to totally leave behind every bit of atmospheric pressure.

Under water, that exponential decrease in atmosphere we found associated with flying (or rocketing) high changes to a direct linear measurement. For every 33 feet under water, the pressure on our body is increased by 1 atmosphere. So, if one was to scuba dive to a depth of 99 feet, the diver would then be subjected to 4 atmospheres of pressure (one we began with at sea level and three more from the dive). Instead of the 14.7 psi, we would now have 58.8 pounds of pressure on every square inch of our body. Therefore, we have a corresponding increase in the amount of nitrogen dissolved in our body fluids, creating a much greater likelihood for the bends to occur if we surfaced too fast. A submarine, 320 feet below the surface, is under almost eleven atmospheres of pressure, meaning that the pressure on the hull is about 160 pounds on every square inch, or, 23,040 pounds on every square foot of the sub's surface.

A submarine in an uncontrolled dive eventually would be crushed like an eggshell at some depth. As long as the integrity of the hull is maintained, the crew inside is safe from that danger. Doctor (Captain) Bond and his research team hypothesized that if a human could get out of a submarine which was disabled at a few hundred feet of depth, he might be able to surface safely without any mechanical breathing gear. Every submarine has an escape trunk (chamber). It's a very small compartment devoid of water and it is pressurized just like the inside of the submarine.

That chamber also has a "sea cock" that, when opened, will rapidly let in sea water. When that chamber is filled with water, one is able to open a hatch to the outside sea and exit. As water fills the chamber, the occupant takes on increasing pressure and the air inside of the lungs compresses to equalize with the sea. Successful escapes had already been made from depths of 150 and 200 feet, but two things had to happen.

Once the crew member left the submarine he would also be under tremendous pressure, the amount depending on the exact depth. That pressure would begin dissolving the nitrogen from the air in his lungs, so speedy action is essential. The idea is to get to the surface as rapidly as is safe. But what is "safe?" Here the second, and probably the most important, function comes into play. As the buoyant ascent occurs and the atmospheric pressure on the body and in the lungs decreases rather rapidly, the air in the lungs also expands rapidly. Holding one's breath during ascent would be fatal. The expanding air in the lungs would, in short time, rupture the lungs. Even though the ascent might take minutes, constant exhalation of the expanding air is essential. The escapee is wearing two items; one is a regular life vest to assist in buoyancy and help carry the person to the surface and the other is a head piece. This is not a breathing apparatus. It simply covers the face and allows the user better vision during the ascent.

In June 1959, the USS Archerfish (submarine) was bottomed off the Florida Keys in 322 feet of water. Captain Bond and three associates readied themselves, entered the escape trunk, and let in the sea water. After seven seconds, they began their ascent, in general, keeping pace with their rising bubbles. The total time from submarine to surface was 53 seconds. All four men reached the surface safely and unharmed.

My training program was quite enlightening and very helpful. Of greatest interest was the use of the decompression chamber, most commonly used for treating the bends.

The underwater testing of the completed Texas Towers Survival Capsule took place in Niantic Bay in Long Island Sound. The "big ball" was loaded onto a very large barge that was equipped with a huge crane. At the appropriate time, the capsule and its concrete base were lifted off the barge and settled in about eighty feet of water. External releases were activated to free it from the concrete anchor, and the capsule immediately popped to the surface. It even leapt several feet out of the water before settling back down.

The next day we readied the equipment for the manned release test. Back on the barge, the crew of seven men was examined before entering the capsule that was in place. The hatch was locked down and the capsule, complete with concrete anchor, was once again lowered into about eighty feet of water. Scuba divers were in place to observe the release from the outside and watch for any problems. I remained on the barge to await the ascent. After about fifteen minutes, the crew in the sphere radioed that they were all strapped in and ready to test the release. On the count, they were directed to "Release."

Nothing happened. Sensing a problem, one of the divers approached the capsule, just as the release mechanism finally did activate and release. The capsule, and the men inside it, were all fine, but about the time they reached the surface, so did one unconscious diver, face down in the water. We retrieved him from the water and I examined him, but was unable to determine if his state of unconsciousness was due to trauma or the bends, and this was no time to guess. I called for a fast power boat and we headed up the Thames River to the Sub Base in New London. The injured diver's pulse and blood pressure were within normal limits. I called Doctor Bond at the Sub Base and he agreed that they should get one of their hyperbaric chambers ready for the patient.

We arrived just at sundown and the diver was immediately placed into the chamber and taken "down" to ninety feet. They proceeded to bring him up according to the Navy Diving Table. He regained consciousness on the way up and told us that as the capsule was being released underwater, he had been hit on the head by something from the capsule. We never did determine whether his unconscious state was caused by the blow to the head or by rapid decompression following the blow. Nevertheless, he recovered completely. In a few months, two of the capsules were installed, one on TT2 and the other on TT3.

12

~ Swinging On A String ~

Serendipity was on the move again for me.

One stormy Saturday morning in the Fall of 1962, I was at home doing weekend chores. Even when the medical offices were not open, there was always a flight surgeon on call to respond to any aircraft emergencies. This was my day. Just before noon, I received a telephone call from the Coast Guard at the Brighten Marine Station near Boston. They said they needed my help, to please meet them at the Otis flight line in twenty minutes, and to bring my medical kit. Suited up and with kit in hand, I was there on time to board their Sikorsky Search and Rescue helicopter. I was briefed as we took off and headed out over the Atlantic Ocean.

It seems a small fishing trawler was floundering in the storm-tossed seas about 150 miles out in the Atlantic. The trawler's captain, who was also the helmsman, had suddenly collapsed and was lying on the deck of the wheelhouse, unconscious and unresponsive. There was poor visibility, low clouds, big waves, and lots of rain—what more could we have asked for? On board our helicopter was a pilot, a co-pilot, a technician of some sort, and the winch-man. And then there was me.

The range of the helicopter was approximately 300 miles and we flew above the clouds to the last known location of the small vessel. Remember, this was 1962, way before GPS became the "in" thing. Our method of finding the trawler was to look for it. We arrived at the approximate position with the chopper's sliding side door fully open. We all peered down through the clouds as best we could. After about fifteen minutes, the pilot announced that fuel was running low and if we did not spot the boat in the next five minutes, we'd have to head back to base.

The five minutes passed without us seeing the boat, but, flying at about 150 feet above the water, occasionally we could catch sight of the waves. The pilot was just calling off the search when one of the crew members thought he spotted something in the water near us. In another few minutes we could identify the fishing boat through the low clouds. On the aft deck, the remaining crew of five were waving wildly to get our attention.

The winch operator readied the cable and quickly fitted the rescue basket, a device made of wire and looking very much like the upper part of a supermarket shopping cart, about 24 inches by 30 inches. The tech's ability to bring up an unconscious victim in that contraption appeared utterly impossible. It seemed, to me, equally impossible just to get the basket onto the 8-feet by 8-feet aft deck of the trawler, given the dreadful conditions of 10-foot waves with rain and poor visibility.

The helicopter itself was also being buffeted in the 30 mile an hour winds. Although I felt the task might be futile, I began to ready the few diagnostic tools I had with me. There was a medium sized oxygen tank and mask attached to the inside of the rear cabin of the helicopter, and it appeared I'd be working from there. It was about that time that I couldn't believe what the pilot was shouting to me.

"What?" I screamed above the storm and engine noise coming in through the large open door. "I said, okay, Doc, into the basket." Still not believing what I think I heard, I yelled back "I'm not trained for this!" He replied, "Just get in, take your bag with you and hang on tight! If the captain is unconscious, none of my men are going to touch him until you've checked him out. And you'd better get going because my fuel gauge says we should be heading home right now!"

This was not the time to be arguing the point. The hoist man helped me into the basket and seated me almost in a fetal position. With my heels against my butt, my bag in my lap (sort of), I put a death grip with both hands onto the steel cables holding the basket to the hook. The hoist arm swung out from the top of the cargo door, supporting me in the basket, and there I "sat" about sixty feet above the churning ocean. The rain soaked me, the wind blew me, and the bobbing boat avoided me.

The first two attempts to get me on the deck failed. They did manage to bounce me off the side of the boat's wheelhouse, though. On the first try, the helicopter shifted to the left while the boat shifted to the right, resulting in a nice dunking next to the boat's hull . . . but I was so drenched from the rain, the sea water really didn't matter. On the third try, one of the boat's crew managed to grab the side of the basket and, with help from two others, held the basket steady while the hoist operator, hanging out of the chopper, played out more cable. Two crewman helped me out of the basket and I was actually able to stand up. The boat was being tossed around in the heavy seas and the crew had to physically guide me to the small wheelhouse.

There I found the trawler's captain lying face down on the deck. I quickly listened to his chest with my stethoscope and then took his blood pressure. Both seemed stable. My mind voted on the probable diagnosis of sixty percent for a stroke, forty percent for a heart attack. Either way, he needed to be hoisted aboard the hovering helicopter to get some of that oxygen into him and on his way out of here. Out on the deck again, I screamed up at the helicopter, "We need to get him up there!" Using a bull horn, the hoist man yelled back, "I don't know if we have time. We may not have enough fuel to get back now!" "You better not leave us here," I threatened. "Give me one minute."

There was a very old, ragged rug on the floor of the wheelhouse. I instructed one of the crew to unhook the basket from the winch hook and another couple to get me several lengths of line. I asked a fourth to help me roll the captain up in the rug, head exposed. We tied strong lines around his chest area, mid-section, and ankles. We then attached the cable hook to the cords around his chest and signaled for him to be hoisted aboard the helicopter.

As our unconscious patient dangled some thirty feet above the water, I prayed that the ropes wouldn't slip. They maneuvered him into the cabin of the helicopter and dropped the cable back down to me. "If we can't get you on the first try, we'll have to come back for you tomorrow—our fuel is critical!" Well, you can bet I had that hook in my grasp within seconds. The boat crew helped me snap the basket back onto the cable hooks and I moved like a veteran getting into that "nest." I was on my way up even before I managed to get a good grip on the basket, but that was okay with me. Actually, I felt pretty good as I was lifted into the chopper and got a smiling thumbs-up from the whole crew. Only then did I realize that during my lift we were actually quite a way from the boat and heading for the cape. There is no question in my mind about what would have become of me had I somehow fallen out of that basket on the way up!

Inside the chopper, we were now able to close the cargo door, unwrap our patient, and start administering oxygen. The pilot radioed the Coast Guard to have a second helicopter standing by to take the patient up to the Boston area. And now we all sat in our respective seats, eyes glued to the fuel gauge. With still a hundred miles to go, the needle was painfully close to the "empty" mark. Even when it hit that mark, we were still about thirty miles from land and the pilot radioed our condition, not that there was much anyone could do about it. Fortunately, there is always a little more fuel, even when the needle is pegged on empty, but no one ever knows just how much that may be. As the pilot quietly said, "I don't think we're going to make it," the tech spotted land ahead through some clouds.

We crossed our fingers and everyone said a silent prayer of their choice. As we passed over the beaches of Cape Cod, the engine began to cough. The airfield was only a mile or so ahead and as we crossed the boundary fence, the engine was *very unhappy*! Rather than have a freewheeling, unpowered descent to our normal parking spot, we landed short of the helicopter pad. We didn't have to shut down the fuel flow—there wasn't any!

The second team took over, moved the patient, and took him away. I never saw or heard of him again but I do know that he survived and may even have made it back to his ocean again.

Evidently, the helicopter crew wrote a report of the whole incident and included some good words about me and my part in the rescue. I believe the "extreme" shortage of fuel was downplayed a bit. A few days later, an article appeared in the Boston newspaper and included this quote:

> *"The flight involved the risk of running out of fuel on the 300 mile round trip over water. Only a few minutes could be spared as the helicopter hovered over the fishing boat while Doctor Enders was lowered by basket and hoisted his patient. The stricken fisherman had been in a coma for three hours. Upon returning to Otis with the man, the pilot had just a few minutes of fuel remaining aboard the craft."*

JRSDAY, MAY 14, 1964, OTIS NOTICE, PAGE THREE

Otis Doctor Nominated For Life-Saving Award

An Otis doctor, one of 23 responsible for the health of America's astronauts via telemetry when they orbit the earth, has been nominated for the Sikorsky Aircraft Company's Winged "S" life-saving award with three U.S. Coast Guard helicopter crewmen.

The award is for saving the life of a heart attack victim on Apr. 18 aboard a fishing vessel more than 150 miles out at sea.

Captain (Dr.) Lawrence J. Enders, an aero-space medical monitor for the NASA space program, is assigned to the 551st USAF Hospital here. When not on duty with NASA, the 33-year-old physician is chief of the Otis aero-space medicine service.

Coast Guard colleagues who flew the helicopter in the humanitarian effort are Lieutenant Roger Frawley, pilot; Lieutenant (jg) Alex Klimshuk, co-pilot; and Aviation Electrician First D.G. Wheat, crew chief, all of Salem, Mass.

Highlights of the crucial flight involved the risk of running out of fuel on the 300-mile round trip over water. Only a few minutes could be spared at sea as the chopper hovered over the fishing boat while Dr. Enders was lowered by basket hoist to his patient.

The 42-year-old fisher- man had been in a coma for about three hours.

Upon returning to the Otis hospital with the stricken man, the pilot had just minutes of fuel remaining.

Rear Admiral C. L. Harding, commanding the First Coast Guard District in Boston, said in commending Dr. Enders, "His on-the-scene assistance was paramount in saving this man."

Capt. Enders

Boston newspaper story on rescue of fisherman

Shortly thereafter I received a congratulatory letter from the Coast Guard Admiral and a lot of thanks. He also sent a copy to the Air Force General commanding our area of Air Defense Command, and then everybody jumped on the bandwagon, including our Base Commander and my boss, the Hospital Commander. A congratulatory letter from the Sikorsky Helicopter Company arrived along with a certificate awarding me the Winged "S" pin, which is given to crew members of Sikorsky helicopters who have saved a life under extremely dangerous conditions.

Not long thereafter, I was selected to play my "bit part" in the Space Program. A letter to my Hospital Commander started as follows:

> *From:* The Department of the Air Force to Area Command
> *Dated:* 19 February, 1963
> *Subject:* Project Mercury, Aeromedical Monitors
>
> *The Department of Defense has pledged continuing support of the Nation's Man-In-Space Program and has asked the three Military Services to assist them in obtaining additional qualified medical personnel to serve as Aeromedical Monitors (later Aeromedical Flight Controllers).*
>
> *The Surgeon General United States Air Force, in support of this request, has again selected certain specialists in aviation medicine who he considers fully qualified to perform this service. Their names have been submitted to the National Aeronautics and Space Administration (NASA) Manned Spacecraft Center, Houston One, Texas, for their consideration. Out of the original list of names forwarded by the Surgeon General, Captain Lawrence J. Enders, USAF, MC, 55762A, 551st USAF Hospital, Otis Air Force Base, Massachusetts, of your Command has been selected for participation in Project Mercury and future Man-in-Space Programs.*

Otis Air Base Surgeon Is One Of 23 New Space Medical Officers

BEDFORD, MASS., MAY 26, 1963

The Standard-Times Cape Cod Bureau

OTIS AIR FORCE BASE, May 25 — Early tomorrow morning a 31-year-old flight surgeon attached to base hospital here will don civilian clothes and head for Logan International Airport in Boston.

There Air Force Captain Lawrence J. Enders, a native of St. Paul, Minn., will board a commercial airliner headed for NASA's Manned Space Craft Center in Houston, Tex., and a week-long debriefing on Astronaut L. Gordon Cooper's 22-orbit flight.

The 6-foot 2-inch flight surgeon is one of medicine's "new breed."

A graduate of Marquette University in Milwaukee and Marquette Medical School, Dr. Enders had a four-month taste of general practice before being tapped by the Air Force in 1957.

Applies for Residency

Once in Air Force blue, the young doctor applied for a three-year residency in aerospace medicine.

As part of his training in medical problems of space travel, Dr. Enders and other residents learned to fly jets ". . . up to the solo point."

Last July, he was assigned to Otis for duty.

His "second hat" was picked up last February when he received orders for an additional duty assignment as one of 23 medical officers of the three armed services assigned to NASA's manned space program.

Shortly before Cooper's shot, the "new 23," who will gradually replace "old medics" assigned to the program since its beginning, went to Houston and Cape Canaveral.

"We studied the capsule environmental controls and the systems control—everything affecting the health of an astronaut," the space surgeon said.

"I spent a whole afternoon in Cooper's capsule. Surprisingly, it was very comfortable.

"Of course, you do have to make a sharp right hand turn to settle in, but once you're in place there's no problem," the doctor said, flashing an enthusiastic grin.

Is he ready to make the first moon shot?

"I'm ready, but I don't know whether they're ready for me," he said. Then he had a second thought, deciding perhaps he'd better wait for the second trip.

But Captain Enders is looking forward to the next manned space junket as much—if not more so—than the astronauts who hope to make it.

He'll be "going along" on the next shot from one of the tracking stations scattered around the world.

Medic Is Assigned

"A medical officer is assigned to each tracking team to monitor medical data," he said. "We also serve as back-up for the systems monitor. On one launch a systems in contingency landing areas in the event an astronaut needs medical help when he lands.

Has Interest in Space

Whatever their duties, the medical officers—if Dr. Enders is typical—have one thing in common: An avid interest in space travel.

During his last trip to Houston, Dr. Enders picked up a souvenir for his 10-year-old son, Stephen, a rabid space fan.

"Gordon Cooper was at the pool at our motel one day and I had a chance to talk to him," Dr. Enders said. "I told him it was my son's birthday and he gave me this to bring back to him."

"This" was an autographed picture of the smiling astronaut inscribed "Best wishes to Stephen."

The doctor grinned when asked if Stevie had managed to watch the Cooper flight on television.

Boy Has Fever

"It just so happened that the day Cooper was supposed to go up, Stevie worked up a fever and had to stay home from school. He managed to hold on to it the next day, too, so he saw the whole thing."

DR. LAWRENCE J. ENDERS

Newspaper article on selection of new doctors for astronauts

Subsequent paragraphs noted that I would be alerted for a period of 1 April through 31 May, 1963, to receive training during the next Mercury flight. It also noted "The precise time involved away from his normal duty station (Otis AFB) cannot be determined for Captain Enders." In other words, don't count on him being around for any specific dates. The letter was signed: *For the Chief of Staff by Major General Richard Bohannon USAF, MC.*

My NASA training was accompanied, on May 26, 1963, by a good-sized article in the Boston paper, headlined, *"Otis Air Base Surgeon is one of 23 new Space Medical Officers"* . . . and not a bad photograph with it.

Command Flight Surgeon of the Year—1962

Arriving that same week was a letter from Air Defense Command Headquarters, Colorado Springs, Colorado, announcing to the 26th Air Division (under which our Base served) that "Captain Lawrence J. Enders was selected as the Command Flight Surgeon of the Year for 1962" and it went on with congratulatory letters, a certificate, high ranking officers making a presentation and more photos in the paper (just in the northeast area).

Somehow the news spread to the north central area of the country because there was an article in the Saint Paul newspapers. Shortly after, I received a letter of congratulations from the Dean of my Medical School at Marquette University, Milwaukee, Wisconsin.

13

~ Spacemen & Pilots & Presidents, Oh My! ~

I was in and out of the base and down at the flight center at Cape Canaveral most of the time for my training. On one of my "study trips" I had been given a stack of manuals having to do with the Environmental Control System of the Mercury Capsule, amongst other subjects. Lodging was at a nice motel at the Cape. On one afternoon, I was sitting alone near the pool reading my manuals. After awhile, I was aware that somebody had pulled up a lounge chair perhaps ten feet from me. There was no one else around.

The new arrival called over to me and said, "You're new around here, aren't you?" I said, "Yes, I am." He asked, "What do you do"? My reply was, "I am one of the new Aeromedical Flight Controllers, catching up on the Capsule." The man jumped up, came over to me, stuck his hand out and said, "Hi! I'm Gordo Cooper. Glad to have you aboard."

We chatted for about ten minutes. He asked me about my family and kids. I mentioned that my oldest son had faked a fever just so he could stay home and watch a recent launch. Gordo jumped up and, with a big smile, said, "I bet you'd like a signed picture of me, wouldn't you?" "Uh. sure," I said. He asked, "What's your son's name? I bet he'd like a picture of me too, wouldn't he?" I answered, "Yes, I'm sure he would." Then Astronaut Cooper ran off to one of the rooms and came back with two photos. The one for me was a picture of the original seven Mercury Astronauts, still in their respective service uniforms, and it was nicely signed by Gordo himself. My son's picture was just of Gordo with the inscription, *"Best wishes to Stephen, Gordon Cooper"*.

Seven original Mercury astronauts
(signed by Gordon Cooper)

Meanwhile, back at Otis where I had spent maybe half of my time, things were going along as usual. Every couple of weekends, especially in the summer, Air Force One settled down on our tarmac, and the Kennedys, along with Secret Service and staff members, would hit the ground on their way to the Kennedy Compound a few miles away at Hyannis Port.

J. F. K.'s Air Force One—Otis Air Force Base, Massachusetts

We played a larger part than expected in our small hospital on the base. The Kennedy Compound consisted of six acres along the Nantucket Sound waterfront. It contained the home of the father, Joseph P. Kennedy, and the homes of John F. (Jack) and brother Robert. During his presidency, it was Jack's Summer White House. The family gathered there most weekends and, amongst other events, would set up the family football grounds. Because of the frequency of the presidential group being there, the Secret Service had to monitor the entire area before each arrival.

Our hospital at Otis, being on a closed base, was the best place to go if immediate care was required. There was no other reasonably-sized hospital in the area should a medical emergency occur. As a result, the Secret Service had to be assured of our security and make sure that a proper staff was on board whenever the Kennedy family was in town. Some personal doctors usually traveled with the President. For example, Janet Travell was the President's back specialist, and she was almost always traveling with him. But when things were quiet on the Compound, she would often come to the base and have discussions with our medical staff.

Clint Hill was also a frequent visitor with us. He was Jackie Kennedy's personal Secret Service man. His most noteworthy photos were seen on the occasion of President Kennedy's assassination in Dallas, when he climbed up the back of the moving Presidential limousine and threw himself on top of Jacqueline just after the first shot hit the President.

Our action picked up significantly when it became known that the First Lady was pregnant for the third time. Caroline and John John were going to have a sibling. After that information came to us, so did Doctor John Walsh, Jackie's obstetrician. He examined our facility and made sure we had all the necessary equipment should Mrs. Kennedy go into labor at an unexpected time. Our hospital at Otis was known as a cantonment-type hospital consisting of only one floor with multiple connecting wings. One wing had been closed down and was, at that time, mostly being used as a storage area. That wing was renovated when the possibility of a Presidential offspring was realized.

As Serendipity would have it, I was on call the afternoon the Washington Post newspaper called for information. The next day the Post came out with an article quoting Dr. Lawrence Enders about the wing. I really don't recall saying 75% of what the newspaper quoted me as saying. But it was in the newspaper, so it must be true, right?

Jacqueline Kennedy was an active woman and an avid equestrian. She was also an active mom to her two children. My family and I were at a local county fair on the Cape one Saturday and saw a sight that is burned into my memory. It was all I could do not to laugh at the sight of Clint Hill holding a melting chocolate ice cream cone that was dripping down his sleeve. Jackie was with Caroline, who was wearing a cute little dress, and John John had on a yellow jumper with a blue duck, all covered with chocolate ice cream drippings. Clint looked at me as if to say, "Don't you say one word!"

We just walked by and politely nodded.

On August 7, 1963, the medical group got a call that Jacqueline Kennedy was on her way to our hospital. All of our doctors were put "on ready" and Doctor Walsh arrived with Jacqueline Kennedy in early labor. The "Kennedy Wing" was activated. It had a patient's room, a waiting room with a doctor, and a few other rooms. This labor was five-and-a-half weeks earlier than expected. The fetus was distressed and an emergency Caesarean section was unavoidable. Doctor Walsh had control and he and our OB specialist scrubbed in. The rest of us were "gophers," but important in the process. The C Section was performed and Patrick Bouvier Kennedy was born, weighing four pounds ten-and-a-half ounces.

His breathing was very distressed, and he was placed on oxygen and immediately transferred by ambulance to Boston's Children's Hospital. The diagnosis was Hyaline Membrane Disease, which blocks the body's ability to transfer oxygen in the lungs to the vascular system and into the body. The same hyperbaric chamber used to treat altitude and diving bends is the best emergency treatment for the immediate crisis. It forces the necessary oxygen into the blood stream but, unfortunately, does not cure the basic problem. It's most commonly found in premature children.

Patrick expired at the Children's Hospital on August 9. Three months later the President was assassinated.

The First Lady stayed in our facility for almost a week. Her personal secretary, also her personal assistant, Pamela Turnure, was a pleasure to work with. The President was appreciative for all the service provided in spite of the sad outcome. He personally thanked the staff as they were all leaving.

The biggest problem, of course, was the Press. They literally invaded the hospital and took over the phones in the offices. One afternoon during the First Lady's confinement, I had a military patient to see. Coming into my office, I found a nationally-known newsman at my desk using my phone, making himself comfortable with his paperwork strewn over my desk. I asked him to leave because I had a patient. He asked me if *I* knew who *he* was? I told him I did, but I still had a patient to attend to. He uttered a few unrepeatable remarks and went stomping off telling me I'd be hearing about this. I never did.

My training with NASA continued and I met more of the Astronauts, sometimes at the Cape and sometimes in Houston at post-flight cocktail parties. One night at the Manned Space Flight Center, there was a well-attended cocktail party. For what, I don't remember. There was a large open bar, but it took a strong NFL lineman to break through the crowd to get a drink. These were my "younger days" when martinis were the drink of choice. My glass was empty and I was surveying the wall of people in front of me when an exceptionally beautiful blonde woman in a long, white, sheath dress asked me if I was drinking martinis. I told her I was, and she asked if I'd be kind enough to get "a lady a drink." She handed me her martini glass, and I forged ahead into the mob.

About ten minutes later, armed with two martinis, I headed towards the woman who was now talking to a gentleman who looked vaguely familiar. I don't know what kind of look I had on my face, but the gentleman looked at my name tag, grinning, and said, "Hi, Doc. I'm Wally Shirra. Don't worry. My wife does this all the time. She gets more drinks that way. Welcome to NASA." We talked for a few minutes and then I drifted off, hoping one of our prized Astronauts didn't think I had been hitting on his wife!

14

~ Astronauts Are Only Human ~

The Mercury Program came to an end and I was requested, again by formal letter, to stay on board for the Gemini Program. I was also transferred from Otis AFB to the Aerospace Medical Center at Brooks AFB in San Antonio, Texas. There I was made Chief of Flight Medicine under the Clinical Sciences Division. From Brooks, it was fairly easy to drive to the Houston Manned Space Flight Center.

The NASA duties were now taking me to more distant destinations. In both the Mercury and Gemini (two-man) Programs, we were seeing manned space flights in their infancy. We didn't really know how extended flights might be endured and tolerated. As a result, the early groups of astronauts were "wired for sound" when they went up, and they were watched by at least a station or two almost every second. NASA had a system of tracking sites located all around the world, in such places as Bermuda; Kano, Nigeria, below India; Perth and Woomera in Australia; Hawaii; Guaymus, Mexico; and even in Corpus Christie, Texas.

Where ground stations were not possible, NASA had its own Navy. Two tracking ships, which could be moved to wherever there was a gap in data collection, solved that problem. The ships were the *Rose Knot Victor* and the *Coastal Sentry Quebec*. Over the next several years, I served at many of these stations monitoring the physiological data of the astronauts, as well as the environment on the spacecraft. I also did my monitoring and communicating from both ships, one time on the *RKV* in the South Pacific, and on the *CSQ* in the East China Sea.

Aeromedical Flight Controllers on Rose Knot Victor tracking ship

Larry on board Coastal Sentry tracking ship

We worked as a team on the flight control missions, usually four of us at each monitoring site around the world. There was the Cap Com (Capsule Communicator) who headed the team, and he was also the final decision maker (go/no-go) after talking to the astronauts and receiving input from the rest of the team. Then there was the Systems Engineer, who monitored the myriad of instruments and mechanisms that made the space capsule livable and assured they performed their required functions.

Flight Controller's consoles aboard the CSQ

There was a communications tech who always made the first contact with the astronauts establishing clear communications, and ensuring that the data from their instruments reached earth. And last, but certainly not least, was the Surgeon or Aeromedical Flight Controller—me. My job was to both monitor and analyze the astronauts' electrocardiograms and follow their blood pressures, heart rates, and body temperatures. Following that, I needed to ask the astronauts how they felt, and to log the quantities of any food or water they may have consumed. My job also included tracking the environmental control system in the capsule itself—its temperature, its oxygen content, and its CO_2 levels. If all was well, we would, individually and as a team, give Houston the "thumbs up" . . . meaning that the mission was still a "go."

Things have changed a lot since the early flights—this was no "joy ride" for the original seven, or even for the next several generations of astronauts. In the more recent shuttle flights, we see pictures of astronauts wearing only their jump suits, smiling and doing tricks for their earth-bound TV audience. However, the early flights required the pilot/astronaut to remain strapped in his seat, to never take off his protective spacesuit, and to eat "dinner" out of a toothpaste tube. They were wired for electrocardiographic monitoring and wore blood pressure cuffs for the entire flight. Rectal thermometers were installed before they entered the capsule.

The pressure in both the cabin and suit was maintained at 5.1 psi, which meant the atmosphere in the capsule had to be 100% oxygen. The cabin temperatures on the first few flights fluctuated between 90° Fahrenheit and 104° Fahrenheit. Fortunately, suit coolers helped with that. Each orbit took around ninety minutes to complete.

Because the earth is spinning beneath the spacecraft, it could only pass over the same monitoring site a few times and then other stations would have to pick up the data. I am very pleased to have a transcript of everything said, to and from the capsule and to the ground, for the first and second Mercury flights, along with all the medical and engineering data, all in one book. Great to have in the memorabilia section of my home library.

It was essential that the original seven not be very tall since the Mercury capsule was only fourteen feet long and six feet in diameter. Even in the Gemini Capsule (two-man flights), Gordon Cooper equated his Gemini V flight experience, with Astronaut Pete Conrad, as similar to two guys *living in the front seat of a Volkswagen Bug for eight days*! Think for a moment, and imagine all the physiological experiences of life they had to share.

I think some of the American public harbored a lot of misconceptions about the astronauts as "men." Often we tend to think of our heroes as supermen, almost indestructible, and with no faults or defects. The astronauts, as brave and courageous as they have been, are, after all, merely human. Not that the public had any need to know, but most Americans never heard about the physical maladies that were just as common with the astronauts as any other group of generally healthy men. Gallstones had to be removed from one. They came down with colds and flu like most people do, although the crew members, for some period prior to a flight, were relatively isolated from potential germ carriers. A number of highly-trained astronauts still got nauseous and vomited shortly after attaining orbit, unaccustomed to the zero gravity state. Medical kits were installed in almost all of the later flights after Gemini.

And, of course, the astronauts were subject to the fatalities that often accompany experimental programs. Each flight "pushed the envelope" a little more. Each flight was preparatory for the next scheduled step in the program. And what is mechanical can, and usually will at some time, fail. As of 2004, eighteen astronauts worldwide had lost their lives during space missions. Four were Russian, thirteen were American, and there was the one Israeli who was on board the shuttle Columbia.

Most of the world heard about some of the astronauts who were killed doing other NASA duties. The big fire on board Apollo 1 during a ground test killed Virgil (Gus) Grissom, Ed White and Roger Chaffee. Elliott See and Charlie Bassett were killed at a fog-covered St. Louis airport, flying in to confer with MacDonald Douglas aircraft people. Ted Freeman crashed in Houston when, on final approach to the airport, a wild goose crashed through the canopy windscreen of his jet. And, because they were human, eight additional American astronauts died in non-NASA related plane and/or car crashes. One died from cancer.

The Russians were not immune from being human either and lost one cosmonaut during surgery and another to an inoperable brain tumor. Some of the astronauts loved the limelight. Others loved their job but avoided publicity and notoriety. I was particularly impressed with people like Rusty Schweikart who had a Master's Degree in Aeronautics/Astronautics from MIT. He flew on Apollo 9 and spent one hour and eight minutes in EVA (Extra Vehicular Activity). That means he was dangling in space, just hooked onto the outside of the Apollo capsule by a few cords and hanging onto the outside handrails.

At another evening cocktail gathering at the Manned Spacecraft Center with the astronauts and other dignitaries, Rusty and I found ourselves uninvolved in group chatter. Rusty looked at me and said, "Hey, how about we slip out and go get a drink at some quieter place?" I was good for that and we hopped into his car and went about a mile away to a quiet bar. We sat in a booth and just "hung out" without paparazzi or "groupies." He was that kind of guy.

On the whole, most of them were, and are, good men. It is an extremely dangerous occupation. But these crewmen are confident in the technology and engineering that goes into every system on board the spacecraft. They, just like the group I flew with in South East Asia, firmly believe that if something "untoward" should befall a crew, it'll always be one of which they are not a part. I'm honored to have pictures and personally signed cards from almost all of the first four groups of Astronauts.

My NASA duties only took part of my time while I was at Brooks. This was mostly just before, during, and then immediately after a space flight. Quite often there were several weeks between the missions, and the Air Force always found something "special" for me to do. I was a board-certified specialist in Aerospace Medicine with a very high security clearance. These two factors made me "fair game" for some unusual assignments.

Pictured on the following page:
(top) The second group of astronauts; (middle left) Gus Grissom;
(middle right) Colonel John Glenn, Astronaut;
(bottom) Sample of the signature cards from the first three groups of astronauts

82

15

~ There Really Isn't A Candy-Striped Pole Up There? ~

Out of the "blue" I received a set of orders sending me off for seventeen days to Hanscom Field in Massachusetts. On arrival, I was directed to attend a briefing with a flight crew for what was called a "very long mission." I'll tell you right now, that mission took me from the Arctic to the Antarctic and to about a dozen points in-between. In addition to the flight crew, comprised of a pilot, co-pilot, navigator, and myself, there were five men in civilian garb. Three were from the Massachusetts Institute of Technology (MIT), and two from the Cambridge Research Institute. The plane we were flying was a significantly modified KC-135 (airborne refueling tanker).

Mission modified KC-135

Ruby lasers inside the KC-135

There was no "deliverable" fuel on board. Instead, in the hold of the aircraft, there were four very large Ruby Laser Generating Machines. Each one aimed out through newly installed, thick quartz, round windows, three on each side of the fuselage.

Not being a physicist, I had no idea of their purpose. Our route of flight, which indeed did go from the exact North Pole down to the edge of Antarctica, generally followed the 70° West Longitude line. Stored on the plane were nine fur-lined Arctic coats. Our mission as a flight crew can very accurately be described as "flying in circles and boring holes in the sky." An explanation of the mission was obviously due the flight crew, but whether we got the whole truth or not, only the five civilians in the back really knew.

The information we were given was this:

> *This was 1965 and the Cold War was dragging on. The USSR and the US were carefully watching each other, quite often via data satellites orbiting in space. Some of those satellites were programmed to detect ground missile launches.*

I believe they picked up the big flare of flame produced by the initial ignition of the booster rocket. It seems that detection problems arose if there was a heavy cloud layer between the launch site and the detecting satellite. The flame might be detected after the rocket passed through the cloud layer, but that may not be until it reached twenty or thirty thousand feet. This, of course, would mean the loss of a minute or two in our response time, and that was totally unacceptable. We needed to "see" the launch the very second that the booster rocket ignited at ground level.

I have no idea about how the lasers fit into the program and I never did find out. However, it seems that for this project we needed to fly from several selected airfields through a series of large circles at several different altitudes. During our circling flight time, the scientists would aim their lasers at "whatever" and then record information on very large on-board data receivers. We started our flight from Massachusetts and headed for our first stop, Thule, Greenland.

70° West longitude

The airbase there is about seven hundred nautical miles above the Arctic Circle and only 550 miles from the magnetic North Pole. It had received some notoriety in January of 1968 when a Strategic Air Command B-52, carrying four hydrogen bombs, crashed into North Star Bay, seven and a half miles west of the air base. On our mission, flying in over North Star Bay for a landing was beautiful.

Glacier in the Arctic from KC-135

The water was filled with "growlers," very small ice flows and icebergs. We spent two days there, sleeping inside of inverted, walk-in freezers. These kept the heat in and the freezing temperatures out.

"It was cold in Greenland".

We started our circular flights in the local area and then moved on to the North Pole. I took pictures of the ice directly over the Pole and was disappointed that there was no evidence of a large spiraling red-and-white pole in the ice. Next, I'll probably find out there is no Santa!

Obviously, after that day, the only direction we could go was south. After sorties out of Goose Bay, Labrador, and Homestead Air Force Base, Florida, we continued heading south passing over the Panama Canal. Our next stop was Guayaquil, the largest city in Ecuador, situated on the west bank of the Guyas River. It was a scheduled stop for us, though we ended up staying an extra day or two.

Returning after the first day of sorties from Guayaquil, we received a radio message from the U.S. State Department. It seems that the daughter of the U.S. Ambassador in Ecuador had come down with a fever, and the ambassador had asked the State Department if there were any American physicians in the country at that time. The State Department checked and replied, "Yes, there is only one. He's an Air Force Captain currently on short stay in Guayaquil." Guess who?

The State Department requested that I fly up there to assess the medical situation. I use the term "up there" because the ambassador and his family lived in the Ecuador capital, Quito. Quito, a city of several million people, is located on the eastern slope of Pichincha Strato Volcano (active). In fact, Quito, with its city square at an altitude of almost ten thousand feet, is surrounded by eight volcanoes. The latest major eruption was in 1987, with its epicenter about fifty miles south of the capital. One thousand people were killed near the epicenter.

Regardless, I was on my way to Quito, but our plane was too big and heavy to land in the mountains. The Ecuadorian Air Force came to the rescue and took me there in an ancient (even back then) DC-3 twin-engine prop aircraft . . . no frills attached. The inside of the DC-3 was stripped bare. Two metal benches were attached to the inside walls of the fuselage, and there I sat. The plane leaked at the seams a bit and, of course, there was no such thing as oxygen on board. But we did have "air conditioning," as the two pilots had their cockpit windows open!

I mention oxygen only because in the U.S. Air Force, one must wear an oxygen mask if flying over ten thousand feet. Although the city square in Quito is just under ten thousand feet high, an aircraft must fly at an altitude of at least thirteen thousand to get over the mountains and volcano peaks before landing at the city airport.

During the flight I was not exactly thrilled to see the pilots did not wear masks; but what I found to be even more disturbing was they both lit up cigarettes at about twelve thousand feet, cutting their own ambient oxygen considerably. Usually, there is very little about flying that bothers me, but to me this was bad news.

Nevertheless, and in spite of the smoking, we landed (sort of) in San Francisco de Quito, which is the full name of the capital of Ecuador. The gods were smiling! I had arrived at my destination alive and there was good news awaiting me. The girl's fever had broken and she was no longer in need of any serious medical treatment. That meant I could return to Guayaquil.

I was wondering if there was a bus I could take for the return journey! That seemed to be a viable consideration for a safer means of traveling. Unfortunately, Guayaquil was hundreds of miles away. Timewise, it would be faster to fly. Besides, how could I resist the adventure of a take-off from the bowl of the volcano at night, flying over the mountains with the two smoking addicts! Later that night, I found our crew having a few beers in the hotel bar so I joined them. Did I have a good story to tell them!

Our next stop was Santiago, the beautiful, huge capital of Chile, with the snow-covered Andes as a backdrop. We stayed in a downtown hotel and had a rental car to get to and from the airport which was located on the northwestern corner of the city ring. We flew from there for two more days, and then down over Punta Arenas and out over Cape Horn into the Drake Passage, before turning back. We had crossed the Antarctic Circle and were quite near Antarctica. We had finished our trek south and, in two more days we would return north with only a couple of stops along the way. At this far point we had a full day of rest coming up in Santiago. So tonight we would celebrate—and we did!

Our aircraft pilot was also our rental car pilot. We had visited several of the pubs that we had been told we just shouldn't miss—and we didn't miss many! By midnight I felt it was safer to sit in the backseat of the vehicle as our fearless leader was feeling no pain; and the more anesthetic he consumed orally, the more he found life enjoyable. Most of the people we met that night were in the same frame of mind, with the exception of the

Santiago Police Department. It seems we were driving, about 1 a.m., on a one-way street going the wrong way. We probably could have gotten off as "out of country men" unfamiliar with this city *if our driver hadn't breathed on the officer and tried to be funny.* When the policeman sternly informed him that this was a "one-way street," he came back with a big smile and said, "What's the problem, my good man? We are only going one way!" At the police station, the US Embassy was called and, although decidedly unhappy about it all, bailed us out. We decided it was wisest to leave Santiago one day early.

There were two more stops on the way home, the first at a base in the Panama Canal Zone, and again a refueling stop at Homestead, Florida. By the time we reached the Boston area, the scientists had gathered all their data, smiled, shook hands, and left. My problem was, what do I tell my boss I was doing for seventeen days?

Upon returning to Brooks AFB and the School of Aerospace Medicine, I found requests for me to speak at both Brown University and the University of New Mexico. The subject was "The Medical Aspects of Space Flight." I enjoyed doing this, and always the most popular and enjoyable part of the talks was my very animated and theatrical reiteration of Gordon Cooper's description of how an astronaut must proceed in evacuating his colon in the confines of the Gemini space craft while in a weightless state!

Many people don't realize that each flight in both the Mercury and Gemini series were designed to test, and prove possible, a step that was required to eventually get a flight team to the moon and back. The Mercury series were basic and allowed us to know we could get to outer space and a human could survive there. One could eat and drink there for almost two days and get back safely. Good, but not good enough. Gemini continued the steps, extending the time in space with two astronauts.

For the Gemini IV flight, I was on the tracking ship *Rose Knot Victor* in the southeast Pacific, sailing out of Lima, Peru. The flight by Jim McDivitt and Ed White was a four-day endurance test, and Ed made the first space walk for twenty-one minutes. One had to be able to work outside the confines of the capsule in emergency situations.

I was assigned to the Hawaii tracking site on the island of Kauai for the Gemini V mission. The station sits on the upper crest of Wiamea Canyon. Gordon Cooper and Charles (Pete) Conrad orbited for eight days. This proved that humans could survive in space flight long enough to travel to the moon and back.

Gemini VI encountered a little trouble at lift off. The idea was for Gemini VI to lift off one day and Gemini VII the next day. Then they were to try to rendezvous in space. On the morning that Gemini VI was to lift off, the count down came down to "engine start" and then warning lights came on. Sitting on top of thousands of pounds of rocket fuel, which could blow them into unidentifiable molecules, Wally Shirra and Tom Stafford methodically shut down the launch sequence with the proverbial "nerves of steel," and all was safe again. I was at the Corpus Christie station for this nerve-wracking attempted launch, and very few of us came away dry. The Gemini VI launch was delayed for about ten days to find the "bug."

In the meantime, Gemini VII lifted off safely on December 4, 1965, with Frank Borman and Jim Lovell at the controls. They stayed in space for thirteen days until Shirra and Stafford, in the repaired Gemini VI, had successfully launched eleven days later on December 15, and the two spacecraft did indeed rendezvous, coming within one foot of each other.

The ability to rendezvous was extremely important if we were going to be able to have the Lunar Landing Module return from the moon to the orbiting Apollo spacecraft during the planned moon landing and retrieval flight of Armstrong and Aldrin.

The Gemini spacecrafts were able to find and approach each other, but could they dock together so that astronauts could actually transfer from one vehicle to another?

On June 3, 1966, Tom Stafford and Gene Cernan launched in Gemini IX. On the previous day, an unmanned, augmented target vehicle with a docking adapter, had been launched. The idea was for the Gemini spacecraft to not only rendezvous with the Agena but to lock on to its adapter. They accomplished the docking perfectly, but the adapter failed to lock. Nevertheless, it showed that docking was possible. From the *Coastal Sentry Quebec* ship in the East China Sea, I monitored the whole flight. Our Flight Control team had flown from Houston to Tokyo, Tokyo to Naha, Okinawa, and there boarded our tracking ship for this mission.

16

~ A Real Fly-By-Night Outfit ~

I was directed back to the Air Force full time in 1966. There was a "small conflict" going on in a country called Vietnam, but before I went there, one more "special mission" was given me. We (the Air Force) had "special" missions being flown from the United States to North Africa and to several European countries.

Old C-119's (Flying Boxcars) were being used for these missions which lasted around eleven days. They started out at Kelly Air Force Base, Texas, and my job was to write a report concerning the sleeping quarters and the adequacy of the sleeping patterns of our crews on these missions. Sounds pretty simple and not very exciting, right? The C-119, built by Fairchild in the early fifties, was used extensively in Korea as a transport and for parachute drops. It had only two reciprocating (propeller) engines, and its cruising speed was, at best, 200 miles an hour. It was not a "speed demon" but it had a pretty good cargo capacity.

The Flying Boxcar C-119

This was the aircraft in which I would spend the next eleven days. I had no idea what our cargo was, but the reason I was on board taking notes was that we slept by day, took off, flew, and landed by night. We flew from Kelly AFB in Texas to my old base at Otis to refuel and then across the Atlantic to the Canary Islands, landing just before sun up. We ate and then went to the BOQ (Bachelor Officer's Quarters) to sleep from about 9 a.m. until late afternoon. The two load masters on board slept at the NCO Quarters. After evening dinner, we went to the flight planning room and the NCOs checked out the plane. Our plane was parked by itself on the far side of the field.

About 9 p.m. we departed for a country in North Africa, landing in the wee hours of the morning. Again, we parked on the far side of the field, far away from any other aircraft and flight line activity. The flight crew, pilot, co-pilot, navigator, and myself managed to eat a very meager early breakfast and, again, headed for the BOQ to get some sleep. The load masters finished their work and did the same. Sleeping in a BOQ, normally occupied by day-working (night-sleeping) officers, was noisy during daylight hours, with people in and out of their rooms slamming doors and talking loudly in the hallway.

That evening we took dinner at 7 p.m. and then made our flight plan. We did this same routine for the next several days and nights, stopping in several European countries at about eight different airfields. We finally came to our "far point" in Italy, not far from Venice. The fatigue from flying all night, with interrupted sleep during the day, was taking its toll. A three-day, two-night crew rest was more than justified! We got a car to take us into Venice and to a nice hotel on the Grand Canal, and, finally, a few good nights of rest.

During the day we toured Venice, ate at Harry's Bar & Grill in the evening, and then wandered the small back streets and trattorias. On the last night there, as we wandered about, we seemed to have acquired a fifth crew member. A "lady" approached the four of us and asked if she could be of any "service" to us. We all said, "No, thank you," but she felt we could at least buy her a drink, which we did. She told us her name was Marisa and she followed us around for the rest of the evening, keeping a short distance behind and occasionally pointing out landmarks, but available should one of us change his mind. None of us did. She followed and followed until about 1 a.m., at which time four of us jumped on a water taxi and headed back to the hotel as Marisa stood on the dock, waving and shouting to us, "Goo'-bye hony." What a nice lady to volunteer to show us the city!

Our route back home was the exact reverse of the route we took getting to Italy, and our sleep/fly sequences were almost the same. Coming across the Atlantic we encountered power problems in one of the engines; however, there was no choice but to continue. Late the next morning we arrived at Otis, refueled, and finally ended our mission back at Kelly AFB. I wrote a report concluding that a small, but separate, building should be made available for these crews to facilitate a better quality of sleep, and an all-night meal area should be available to cater to crews arriving and departing at times when the regular mess hall was not open. It was only much later that I found out what "strategic cargo" we were carrying. Let's just call it "fresh" going out, and "depleted" coming back.

17

~ Oh, Rats! ~

After only one month at home, my new orders arrived. The Vietnam conflict had caught up with me. A promotion to Major was also the order of the day. I was to depart on July 31, 1966, for Southeast Asia. I would be met in Bangkok by an administrator of a clinic being built and then flown to U-Tapao Air Base, which was just being carved out of the jungle in the southern part of mainland Thailand. I was to be the director of base medical services there and assist in the building of a small hospital. But before leaving the US, I was required to take some special training in weapons, swamp and foliage familiarity, and a bit of "snake" training. It seems that our new base was a favorite lair for cobras.

As we made our approach for landing in our DC-3, I failed to see very much of the expanding base. That was because it hadn't expanded very much at all. Bulldozers were busy clearing the jungle and laying down a type of ground clay called laterite, especially where there was going to be a nice long runway. I say "going to be" because the completed runway just did not exist at that time. We landed on a taxi-way. My quarters was a very nice "hooch" built for six. An area of jungle had been cleared away, concrete pads were laid down, and wooden-framed tent tops were erected to cover six-bed sleeping quarters.

A collection of "hooches" S.E.A.

At work in my office—U-Tapao Air Base

There was a warped screen door on each end of our hooch and a 3 x 6 foot metal locker stood at the foot of each bed. Welcome to the Waldorf! Of course, no running water or sewage facilities were available. There was, however, one electrical outlet per bed. The "facilities" (latrine and shower) were about one block walking distance away.

The newcomers' briefing started thus:

> *"Place your boots right next to your bed; always have a flashlight in your hand before getting out of bed at night. Always shine your flashlight into your boots before putting your feet into them as snakes like to curl up for warmth inside boots. Never go to the latrine at night without a flashlight. The paths to the latrines are constructed by placing 2 x 4's along the side edges, and filling the area in between with crushed gypsum rock. Always shine your light on the path a good way in front of you, as the sun on a hot day warms the Gypsum and the cobras like to sleep on it at night."*

Everything you owned went into the lockers or you threw it out. Of course, fatigue uniforms and boots were the standard garb. I reported directly to the Group Commander who had a briefing every day for his staff. Colonel Chris was a "by-the-book" man. There were three other doctors there, all of whom reported to me. Our "hospital" was a large tent. I saw my first case of Dengue Fever the next day. The patient had a temperature of 104+ F. There was some electricity available to the "hospital" tent, and we ran a small ice-maker to which we had to bring water each day. It took a few weeks for me to get accustomed to primitive medicine.

Getting settled in, I fell behind in my flying requirements, so I made it up by flying a few support missions over non-combat zones. My administrative officer introduced me to the area in and around the base. Our airfield was, officially, a Thai base on assignment to the United States, but most of the services people on the base, and some guards, had to be Thai.

Just down the dirt road from the base, a number of "bars" sprouted up. Barely more than wooden shacks, they made available beer, liquor and "hostesses" for the GIs. These were all Thai property and I had no jurisdiction over anything off the base. If, however, we had a significant number of sexually transmitted disease cases traceable to a certain bar, we could put it "off limits" to US Military personnel. It was a very "touchy" situation and we needed the cooperation of the local Thai public health personnel. And they were very cooperative.

Once a month, every girl "working" the local bars had to undergo a vaginal smear for the detection of venereal disease. This was conducted at a Regional Public Health clinic several miles down the road. Each bar had sheds out back for the girls to "entertain" their customers and, when not "entertaining," they served drinks in the bar and sought new customers. The local public health nurse took me on an inside tour of the establishments. I must have met a hundred young girls from the local bars. They were almost all quite small and, to their credit, very cordial and well-mannered. By nature, they all looked very young and of a much smaller stature than an American woman of the same age. They were happy and smiling almost all the time.

Their "profession" was perfectly acceptable in their culture. Most were married and many had children, although one would never have guessed that. A great number of them lived in small huts behind "their" bar with their husbands and families. One might wonder how such a situation could be acceptable to the husbands, but good-paying jobs were very scarce in these small, local jungle villages. The truth of the situation was, a "hostess" could, in one night, make more money than her husband, working as a laborer, could make in one month. That was the simple economics of it all.

The girls accepted the medical examination ritual with no argument. If a girl was found to be "positive" for a sexually transmittable disease, she could continue work as a waitress but could not conduct any "back room" business until cured. She received treatment at the clinic and, in addition, had to wear a red name plate on her blouse that read, "I got VD." That was compliments of the Thai public health nurse, who was a toughie. Together, with the Thai Nurse, we could randomly drop into a bar, check the names of the girls with the tags, and then check the clients in the back. If a "restricted" girl was found in the back with a client, the bar would be put "off limits" for one month. So it was economically best—all around—for the bars and the girls to conform to the rules.

In a couple of months I knew most of the girls by their first names. They never used their real Thai names, of course, but made-up American names like Betty, Lyn and Sue, or shortened Oriental names like Gin, Kim and Nan. We only did random checking about twice a month, at different times and in different bars; but, occasionally if we suspected any "game playing" was going on, we'd do the same bar twice. Actually, it was not an unpleasant function and it didn't take too long for all the girls to recognize me. When I would walk into a bar, they would come running over to me, give me a big hug and shout, "Doctor Checky-checky." They would say "Doctor Checky-checky, see my badge."

Some brought their babies out for me to see and, all in all, it was a very relaxed and enjoyable duty. Only twice, early in the program, did a girl offer me "free services" to get her name off the restricted list. I explained that if they offered again, they would be permanently "blackballed." The word got around and we kept to the cordial hugs after that. The villagers were totally different.

A few months into my tour in Southeast Asia, we acquired a very intelligent, English-speaking Thai nurse to work in our clinic on base. We had brought in, as our new clinic, something equivalent to a double-wide mobile home that actually had some windows and an air conditioned room for our inpatient "ward." The new nurse's name was quite difficult to pronounce, so she told us to call her Sophie.

She mentioned a few times how fortunate the people on our base were, to have access to all the medicines we had available. The people in the villages surrounding our base, off the beaten path so to speak, had little access to medical care. When I was not in the clinic taking care of patients or doing my "Doctor Checky-checky" business or flying, I actually had some weekend days off. Sophie asked if we had any interest in visiting some of the closer villages to assess their medical situations. But before we could do anything like that, we had to get the permission of the District Police Chief, who has total control over everything that happens in his area. Even if we went to a village, we could not treat anyone without the permission of the Police Chief.

So, for our first venture into the "back woods," he accompanied our small group consisting of one American nurse, our Thai nurse, and myself. The Chief made a short speech to the village residents (in Thai), to which Sophie cringed a little before translating for us. Basically, the Police Chief told the people how he had managed to convince the American medical people to share their services and medicines with the Thais. Sophie also told me that the Police Chief somehow conveyed that he would be quite open to receiving gifts and gratuities from the people for "his" services.

This particular village was about twenty miles from our air base and maybe two or three miles down a dirt lane from the nearest paved road. There were about twelve dwellings ringed around an open area of packed dirt, in the center of which was a fairly large fire pit. Most of the dwellings were up on stilts with the first floor about six feet above the ground. This level had a railing around it but was otherwise open. Several houses had second floors which were for sleeping. Of course, there was no electricity, running water, or sewerage pipes. There were two gasoline-run generators that provided some light in the village after sundown.

Most households had a few kerosene lanterns of their own. Wooden ladder "stairs" led up to the first levels where there was some simulation of a kitchen with some utensils. Bowls and cooking pots were stored there. Food was "assembled" there although most of the actual cooking was done outside in the common fireplace. Apparently, in rainy weather, small fires were sometimes made in the dirt under the houses themselves. Obviously, there were no OSHA inspectors in the area.

The bathroom facility in each house was on the ground level, under the first floor. Basically, it was a three-sided stall about the size of a telephone booth with a curtain hung on the fourth side as a door. In the center of the floor was a hole about one foot in diameter. I don't know how deep it was, but on top of the hole, a porcelain plate, with a hole in the center and a foot pad on each side, was set in place. There was a water trap molded to the underside of the plate, which hung down into the hole. Beside the bathroom there was a large wooden barrel containing collected rainwater which provided the "flush" and/or shower water. A two-quart plastic bowl floated in the barrel to allow you to either deposit water into the toilet or pour it over your head for your "shower."

I had brought a few antibiotics, as well as some antiseptics and bandages. It seemed that these items were going to prevent or cure about 80% to 90% of all the health problems there. The Police Chief had decreed that our visit would only last two hours. He sat at a small table at one of the better constructed huts and took down the names of all the patients before they could be treated.

Police Chief takes names at the "village"

The villagers were very grateful and expressed hope that we could return. We did. But because of the unpredictable timing of my duties at the base, we could not give them any long-term schedule. Each visit had to be approved by the Police Chief, but after a few times he didn't bother to accompany us anymore. In fact, on several occasions, when our nurses were busy caring for base personnel, I went by myself.

By this time, I had picked up a little of the language and could communicate with some of the people in the villages who spoke limited English. Between the two languages, we managed to make our intentions and needs known to each other. They asked me if occasionally it would be possible for me to stay over on a Saturday night and see more people on Sunday morning. I really needed to be available at the base for part of each and every day but thought that an occasional overnight stay might be possible.

During my first few visits when Sophie had come along, we had been able to do a little Public Health training. We spoke of personal hygiene and lots of washing before preparing foods, and we also emphasized the need for protection from mosquitoes which were in great abundance once the sun went down. Malaria was quite common there, and I was on chloroquine and primaquine all year. One never knows if talks like this get through language and cultural barriers.

It was with great pride that on my first "overnight" visit I was shown my sleeping quarters on the upper floor of one of the better structures where they had built a bed for me (of sorts). It was four 2 x 6 foot boards, nailed together to form a rough rectangle on the floor, about five feet by seven feet. Inside the rectangle was a thatch-filled mat that would be my "mattress." Above the bed, with its tented peak attached to the ceiling timber, hung a mosquito net. It was large enough for me to tuck the edges under my "mattress" to completely seal out the pests. Although each of the four walls had a "window," there was no glass in them—just empty space and the jungle outside.

I don't know what the spokesman's name was, as the pronunciation was more than I could handle. His English was very poor and he mostly delegated the presentation of my quarters to a middle-aged lady (although a woman's age is hard to discern in Thailand). Her name was simple and I could remember it—Mrs. Fuang Fa.

I must mention that my "bed and mattress" were exceptional because, for the most part, the village residents all slept on the floor on small carpets, and they had no protection against the mosquitoes. I thanked them all profusely, bowed from the waist and, with palms together as in prayer, delivered my best "*khop khun, mak*" ("thank you very much") several times. Big smiles all round.

We had a celebratory meal of rice and bits of chicken (I think) from a large wok. Just grab a handful and put it on your plastic plate, and eat it with your hands or spoon-fork. After the meal, the "garbage," that is the left-over food and table scraps, were simply tossed out of the "kitchen" window to be carried off by whatever animals were around at the time. That night I had surprise visitors.

Of course, I slept with my clothes on and with a flashlight by my side. After tucking in the mosquito netting, I eventually fell asleep. Sometime in the middle of the night I was awakened by scratching sounds on the wooden floor. I turned on my powerful flashlight, and from every direction in the room I saw these *brilliant red eyes* reflected in the beam. I sat up in bed, which caused a scurrying from the bodies that owned the red eyes. They were about the length of a big cat and possessed front fangs and a long, "rubbery" tail. I would guess they were jungle rats, each weighing about ten pounds. I clapped my hands and they all took off in different directions. So much for sleep the rest of that night! I suppose that each night they would come in to eat the day's "garbage" scattered around under the huts, but this night they smelled "fresh meat"—*me*!

I continued my village visits when I could. The people there were so warm and grateful. The most heart-warming event came about near the end of my thirteen-month tour when I explained to the villagers that my next visit would be my last and that I would be leaving their country for America. They seemed saddened but happy for me in the knowledge that I was going home to my own family, in my own country. On my last visit I asked Sophie to go with me, as I wanted her to interpret, in Thai, my deep feelings for the people and to thank them for their hospitality.

When we arrived, they had chicken and rice and Singh Ha beer. After we dined, they said their thanks to me and Sophie and asked that it be passed on to the other medical people. Then the Head Man stepped forward and took off a chain he had been wearing around his neck. He handed it to Fuang Fa, who placed it around my neck and told me that it was a Thai amulet which would protect health-giving people from danger—and it was perfect for me. Once again, I thanked them over and over before our departure. I had not inspected my gift there in the village; I just wore it. Back at the base, I took it off in my office and examined it closely.

My gift from the villagers

The amulet itself was carved from a dark brown baked clay, with the resulting figure, then encased in a 24k gold frame. The whole amulet itself looked old, and the back of it was quite well worn from rubbing on someone's body. I asked Sophie about that and found out that if you buy an amulet for yourself, the "blessing" or "power" does not come with it. It must be given to you from someone else who has worn it. It is a token, a way of passing their protection on to another person whom they love or admire. It is not uncommon for amulets to pass down for generations in families. As Sophie was explaining all this to me, I recognized that the heavy chain was also 24k gold. In 1967, this would have cost around $200 to $300 to purchase, just at the gold rate alone. I would expect that now it would be worth a lot more. I told Sophie then, after realizing its value, I couldn't accept such a costly item from the village which had so little. Sophie proceeded to gently reprimand me, saying that the amulet was not purchased and it would have been a gross insult had I not graciously accepted it. It is now one of my prized treasures.

I have researched the amulet since then and discovered that it is a representation of the spirit Pra Leela. The internet states that the "gray, gray-green and brown colors are rare to find items". All the prime materials for making real amulets, namely the prime holy soils, are a mixture of the soils from the following locations: where the Grand Buddha was built, the major temples across the country, and 108 herbs and flowers from respected altars. The soils are blessed for three days continuously before the baking and carving. After the amulet is finished, it is blessed continuously for another three days from May 2-5. How rare mine is I do not know, but the rarer ones are sold by collectors for hundreds of thousands, even millions, of Baht. (Thai money). My Leela's image and its specific pose represents the Abhaya mudra (the hand gesture of no fear). Therefore it represents protection, peace, benevolence, and the dispelling of fear for the wearer. Sophie related to me that the one I have would protect me from danger during my "work" in Southeast Asia. I still have the amulet, and I'm still here. Don't mess with something that's working.

18

~ A Guy Could Get Hurt Doing This! ~

Understand that all these off-base activities were going on intermingled with the increasing medical and combat efforts at the base. From the time I landed on that taxi-way, construction of all functions on the base was going ahead at full speed. After two months, we now had a wooden slat-board Officers Club and an NCO Club. We had a bigger mess hall, and my medical office was moved from my tent to rooms in an addition to the double-wide clinic. Ten beds were now available for inpatients. The new Officers' Club had a relatively long bar and a juke box ("Winchester Cathedral" was the top hit then), and there were several tables and chairs mostly occupied by card players each night.

There wasn't much else to do in any spare time (well, nothing safe that is). Most nights a few of us medical folks would stop in for a beer or almost any other concoction imaginable. Early in my third month there, one night at about 11 p.m., I was sitting at the bar with some friends solving the problems of the world. It was a Friday night, and I specifically remember that because during the week martinis were 25 cents but on Friday nights they were 10 cents. At that stage of the evening, I think I was about forty cents into the night. I knew most of the base pilots by now and as I sat there, it dawned on me that three of the group sitting down the bar from me were on a list for a mission early the next morning.

My "preventive medicine" mode took over and I very gently asked them, "Hey guys, what happened to the adage 'twelve hours between bottle and throttle'"? It was quiet for a few seconds and then a young Lieutenant, I'd say about seventy cents into the night, put his finger on my chest and said, "Doc, we all like you. You take good care of us. But tomorrow all of us here will be up over the north (Vietnam). Most of us will come back but maybe not all of us. When you start flying some of those kinds of missions, we'll drink when you say we can."

There was silence that, to me, seemed to last for hours but was probably only about twenty seconds. And then my "forty cent evening" kicked in and I said, "OK, you're on." Four days later I took my first mission over the north. I wasn't totally stupid, although there was no real consensus about that from my medical cohorts. I told myself I would not take flights where my (or our) aircraft's primary purpose was to kill people, except in self-defense and if we were being fired upon.

My first several missions were in KC-135 refueling tankers. Our job was to follow flights of fighter bombers to an area near their target and stand by to refuel them either just before they went in or just after they came off their strikes against North Vietnamese ground units. These could be anti-aircraft sites or the worst—SAM (Surface-to-Air-Missile) sites. If we had played our hand by the book, we in the refueling plane would circle short of the North Vietnamese border, out of range of anti-aircraft fire or the SAMs, and wait for the fighter bombers to come to us. Each mission I was on started that way. But if we were circling and one of our aircraft called to us that they were almost out of fuel coming off a third or fourth strike, what choice did we have? We would get his position and meet him wherever that was. Sometimes I was in the cockpit with the crew and could see some of the action and other times I was in the refueling pod.

Refueling an F-4

An F-4 on a "Wild Weasel" mission

After enough missions, I actually got to handle the big refueling boom hanging from our underside. I flew on whatever missions I could serve as crew. Of course, the more frequently I flew one type of a mission, the more I got to actually participate as an active crew member. But mixing it up was quite interesting too. Eventually most of the pilots let me have some stick time.

There is this "thing" that seems to happen in a combat zone. People tend to do what "seems" logical at the time but sometimes is not really logical. Some rules and regulations get "bent" a little if it seems to be in the best interest of someone. For instance, when I was doing the weekend village stuff, I was not supposed to take our hospital Jeep off the base overnight. All the guards knew me and just waved me by because it was for a "good cause." And why throw out medications the day they come to their printed expiration date? If ampicillin was good to give on Tuesday, it did not suddenly lose all its potency on Wednesday morning! But Regulations forbade its use in our clinics and said the drug should be destroyed. It is astounding the number of infections in those villages that were cured by these "out of date" drugs. Naturally, I would not have administered them had they expired eight or nine months previously, but most of these meds retained some respectable potency for several months after the expiration date.

But, more about "bending the rules." There were many other bases in Thailand that had Chief Flight Surgeons with the same background and specialty training that I had. We all knew each other—like a "brotherhood." We would call each other on the phone just to check what was going on at the other bases. One week we decided that "in order to coordinate medical programs and processes," we should swap bases for a week. I had my Administrator cut orders putting me on TDY (Temporary Duty Elsewhere) to Nakon Phenom for one week. Nakon Phenom was located very near the Mekong River, just a "stone's throw" from Laos. It was not an illegal thing, but then we may have had some ulterior motives, like swapping mission types. Nakon Phenom (NKP), called "Naked Phaney" by most crewmen in Thailand, was the home for the O-1e Birddog.

The O-1e was a small fixed-wing prop plane built by Cessna. Earlier it was called the L-19A (a Cessna 170 in disguise). The high-winged, simple little two-seater (one in front, one directly behind) had top speed of about 150 miles per hour and usually cruised at a little over a hundred miles per hour.

The O-1e "Birddog"—Forward air controller (FAC)

Used as an observation plane, its mission was as a Forward Air Controller (FAC). It only weighed about 1600 pounds empty and had just one door, which was on the starboard (right) side. It was split horizontally so half swung up and the other half swung down. The front pilot's seat's backrest had to be flipped forward to allow the second crewman to crawl into the back—a bit like climbing into the back seat of an old VW Beetle. My good flight surgeon friend got me all fixed up so that my first mission from NKP would be in the O-1e. There was no armament on these aircraft, but they did carry two white phosphorous marking rockets, one under each wing. My pilot helped me get outfitted because I had never flown this type of mission before.

There was the standard flight suit, boots, helmet, a survival knife, a .38 caliber pistol on my hip, a survival vest with all sorts of gear attached, and some "blood chits." Blood chits were official pieces of paper in several of the languages used in the area, which, in case we went down, guaranteed that anyone helping me to hide from the enemy or get back to safe territory would receive $1,000 from our government. On top of the survival vest went a flak vest. Actually, we each took two flak vests, one to wear and one to put under our seats. Finally, on top of all that, we wore a parachute.

A typical mission would go like this: Shortly after our take off, a squadron of Navy Corsairs from a Carrier in the Gulf of Tonkin would also get airborne. We were in communication with the Navy squadron as we flew across the Mekong at about a thousand feet, towards South Vietnam, and then headed for the Ho Chi Min Trail. The Demilitarized Zone between North and South Vietnam was heavily guarded and blockaded. In order for the North Vietnamese to re-supply their troops in South Vietnam, they would take a truck convoy on an incursion route around the DMZ through Laos.

Laos was not supposed to be involved in this war. Regardless, the truck convoys mostly came around the western end of the

DMZ, through some jungle roads in Laos and then down to the south. This route became known as the Ho Chi Min Trail. Our job then was to fly up and down the Trail, at an altitude of about 100 to 150 feet, and look for truck convoys or other evidence of military hardware being moved through that area. Of course, at that low altitude, we were very susceptible to small arms fire. A good shot from a pistol could do the job, and certainly a rifle or machine gun could bring us down. If we spotted any enemy movement, we were to circle around, come back to the area, and fire one of our phosphorous rockets as near as we could to the truck park or convoy.

Wherever the rocket hit, it would send up a very large cloud of white smoke that would last for several minutes. We would then call up the Corsairs and relay the map coordinates so they could find our "smoke" and then "drop" their ordnance at a designated distance and direction from it. It wasn't necessary for the Corsairs to actually see the convoy. They would drop their loads—bombs, rockets, napalm, whatever they were carrying—on the spot to which we had directed them, virtually obliterating several acres of jungle. In the meantime we got out of the way and observed from a mile or so distant from the action. It wasn't hard to figure out whether the convoy was hit or not. If it was, there were usually many secondary explosions as trucks filled with ammunition, fuel, and other ordnance ignited and then disintegrated.

What I still haven't figured out is, why the parachutes? First, if anything happened to the "front-seater," the flier in the back could never get out of the plane. Secondly, how much good would a 'chute do you (even if you could bail out) at 150 feet! But it was not my job to question such things. That was way above my pay grade!

I am sure you are wondering about the wisdom of the mission plan. At 150 feet, one could easily be shot down. The O-1 crew would be gone, and the Corsairs would never know where to find any enemy trucks. But every question has an answer. After that happened a few times, the strategists redesigned the mission plan and sent two O-1's on each mission. Approaching the suspected area, one of the 0-1's would fly up to six or seven thousand feet (called "high key") while the other took the "low key" route at 150 feet. If nothing was sighted after a certain number of low-level runs, they would switch positions. If the "current" low key aircraft was hit, the high key plane would call in the Corsairs to wipe out the source. I'm not too sure how much consolation that would be to the occupants of the destroyed low key O-1, but then I don't think war considers that essential.

By the time I returned to my original base in the south, I had a total of thirty-five combat missions for my time in Southeast Asia. My flight records reflected this and the head of base operations at my unit put me in for the Air Medal. I knew nothing about that and was pleasantly surprised about a month later when orders came out announcing my Air Medal Award.

An interesting, but maybe not so strange, phenomena happens to people who do potentially dangerous things repeatedly, without harm. They do it again. And again. And soon, it almost becomes routine, with one gradually losing his fears (to a degree) and, sometimes, his good judgment. He forgets the potential for disaster still exists. I occasionally think of Roy from the great Las Vegas show, *Siegfried and Roy*. White tigers, as "sweet" as they may look, are still quite dangerous. Roy got emotionally close to his white tigers and may have forgotten that they are still "wild animals." Perhaps he forgot that while they may lick your hand one day, they could—for no apparent reason—bite it off the next. *In life, you've got to know your tigers!*

I saw this happen to many of our combat crewmen. Anxious at first, then accepting, and then very nonchalant, always holding onto the thought that if one of the squadron's planes did not come back, it was always going to be "someone else," never them.

I guess I wasn't too different on a second, self-initiated TDY to Korat and Ubon Air Bases. From Ubon, I got to fly a ground suppression mission (known as "Sandys") which are flown in two-seater Douglas A1-E's.

A1-E "Sandy" mission

The A1-E is another single-engined prop plane, but much more powerful than the O-1. It carried a gamut of ordnance; machine guns, 20mm cannons, rockets, even small bombs or grenades . . . and a super-powerful Gatling Gun. Its job was to respond to a signal from a downed pilot, locate and identify the flier (in enemy territory) and then to circle him, laying down suppression fire to keep "Charlie" (North Vietnamese soldiers) away from the pilot until a "Jolly-Green" (large rescue helicopter) could fly in and pick him up. Again, the relative slow speed and low altitude of the A1-E mission made it quite susceptible to ground-to-air-missiles. By the time I was near the end of my tour in Southeast Asia, I had already been credited with 75 combat missions and a second Air Medal.

```
                    DEPARTMENT OF THE AIR FORCE
                    HEADQUARTERS SEVENTH AIR FORCE (PACAF)
                         APO SAN FRANCISCO 96307

  TO
  OF:   DPSA

  ICT:  Award of Air Medal, Lt Colonel L. J. Enders, FR55762 (Your
        Ltr, 29 May 69)

  TO:   HQ USAF (AFIAS-L)
        Norton AFB, Calif 92409

        1. Lt Colonel Lawrence J. Enders, FR55762, will be awarded
        the Air Medal with one oak leaf cluster.

        2. Award elements will be forwarded in approximately three
        weeks.

                FOR THE COMMANDER
                                              2
                                              5
                                                    Combat fire
  IP    STUD    CIv    OTH-US   FGN-MIL   GRND-TOT   CMBT   CMBT-SPT
  .2                                       26.2
  .1                                      1990.1    171.5

  MOST CURRENT---
  ICRAFT  FLT   DATE

  ;1a1    73 AUG 15
```

Orders and flight record for Air medal with Oak Leaf cluster

In about the twelfth month, I got a call from the Air Force Surgeon General's office in Washington D.C. Because I was officially a member of the Medical Corps, all administrative paperwork concerning me was run through medical channels. The Surgeon General's office had missed the paperwork awarding my first Air Medal, but not the second one. The phone call was to reprimand me for flying combat missions since the Geneva Convention Rules stated that "no medical personnel could bear arms of any sort." My last month was limited to behind-the-lines flights. Okay, it was a legitimate reprimand, but that did not diminish the esteem I had garnered from the line officers.

Our base and group commanders all congratulated me on the awards. One has to understand that, basically, "line" officers run the Air Force. Of course, all of the Service's military people are essential regardless of their specialty field, but the line officers are the ones who become the squadron commanders, wing commanders, and generals. They, indeed, ultimately run the Air Force. A good word from one of them was worth its weight in gold, and this is especially so for medical officers. Sadly, many medical people are not usually considered to be very "military" by the line officers. Maybe that's because most medical people have a mind of their own and are not the greatest for following orders from someone else, let alone from a manual. It was not uncommon, especially in the doctor-draft years, to see medical people wearing their decorations improperly, their insignia a bit crooked, and their salutes more like swatting flies. I am reminded of the ever-popular and highly irreverent character Hawkeye Pierce in the great TV show, "M*A*S*H."

19

~ Back In The Saddle Again ~

Basically, my tour of Thailand ended happily. My orders called for me to go back to the Aerospace Medical Center at Brooks AFB in Texas. My new position was going to be a step up and, unknown to me until I arrived at my new assignment, my line commander in Thailand had sent a letter to my new boss congratulating him on getting a great doctor and military officer. Not all men scheduled to depart Thailand were as lucky as I was.

It was not unusual for a soldier or an airman who lived for an extended period of time on the "other side of the world" from home to fall in love with a girl native to the country where he temporarily resided. I knew several men who, in fact, moved in with girls, usually from one of the bars, and set up housekeeping. I mentioned that the girls were sweet and very anxious to please, but the problem arises when the military man happens to be married with a family back home in the States. So was the case of one of our sergeants on our base.

It was said that he loved his family at home, but he also loved his new-found woman. It all came to a peak when his tour ended and he received his orders to return to a base in the United States. The Air Force was using both military aircraft and civilian airlines on contract to move troops back and forth. The sergeant's orders directed him to report to Bangkok airport to board a specific plane at a designated time. He had confessed to his friends that he was very upset and that he just didn't know how to handle his feelings. He never showed up at the airport. Some of his friends knew where he lived off base and went to his dwelling. There they found him hanging by his neck from a ceiling rafter. He had chosen a third option. There are all sorts of casualties in war.

My flight back to the United States was uneventful. Everyone on board clapped and cheered when our aircraft touched down in California. From there, we all scattered in different directions. My "personal cargo" was pretty heavy since I had obtained an Akai M-8, with speakers, up in Guam on one of my support missions. Along with that, there were some other things for my family. Back home, and back at the Aerospace Medical Center in San Antonio, life settled down a bit as I became re-oriented to the US.

Shortly after my return, I received an Air Force Commendation Medal for my service in Thailand, along with my Vietnam Service Ribbon. My new superior showed me the letter he had received from the Wing Commander in Thailand, which was very complimentary. My new job was a "one of a kind" position. I was in charge of the Aeromedical Consultation Service.

Every year the government was spending millions of dollars to train new pilots. In the mid-sixties, the cost was calculated to be about $360,000 for each young officer to complete his flight training and get his wings. Flight safety is always a primary concern. Any number of medical problems can result in a flier being grounded. Any ailment that can interfere with a flier safely handling an aircraft is "just cause" for removal from flying status. There are also some medical symptoms, which by themselves, require the immediate grounding of a flier. Just one, for example, is loss of consciousness for any reason. Imagine a group of people standing at attention for an hour in the blazing sun. If someone passes out, that is not too unusual. If that person is a pilot, he is automatically grounded. If a pilot is mugged in some back street somewhere and knocked unconscious, he would also be grounded. These are only two examples.

There are also a number of lesser maladies which may result only in a temporary grounding. These groundings may be able to be reversed by the local flight surgeon after the medical problem clears. A head cold, for example, may be associated with an inability to clear the ears when coming down from altitude. Once the cold has gone, the flier can be cleared by his own base flight surgeon. Regardless, on the Aeromedical Consultation Service at the School of Aerospace Medicine, some 500 to 600 grounded air crew members are seen each year for a thorough evaluation of conditions which might be considered justification for permanent grounding.

I should mention that the Consultation Service, by itself, has no authority to either ground the flier or to return him to flying status. It "recommends" based on a thorough investigation of the flier's medical condition. After being evaluated for four or five days at the "Service," the resultant recommendation is sent to the flier's flight surgeon on base, to the Major Air Command Surgeon under which the flier serves, and to USAF Headquarters in Washington. Historically, it is a rarity that our recommendations were ever reversed by a higher authority.

The evaluation process worked like this. The Consultation Service had twenty five BOQ (Bachelor Officer's Quarters) rooms set aside at Brooks for incoming examinees. In my first year as Chief, I saw 540 fliers. I first reviewed the complete medical history of each patient in order to understand the medical aspects for grounding the individual. I would then order a complete laboratory screening which included a thorough blood screen and glucose tolerance test. This was followed by electrocardiograms, electroencephalograms (if there was anything neurological suspected), a body composition study, chest and abdominal X-rays, urinalysis and an audiogram.

If it was suspected that there were any cardiovascular elements involved, a treadmill stress test was scheduled. The Consultation Service had, at that time, two F-100 high-performance jets, that would enable us to take a flier up in the air. He would be totally wired so we could study any cardiac or vascular changes along with his current G load tolerance. Attached to the "Service" we had one or two specialists in almost every field of medicine. These included ear/nose/throat specialists, cardiologists, psychiatrists, neurologists, orthopedic specialists, internists and ophthalmologists. You name it, we had it.

After the preliminary physical examination and lab evaluation, our staff team would work out a more specific evaluation program determining which specialists needed to see the patient. Each morning our group met and discussed the progress of each patient. Each of the specialists' evaluations would come to me when their exams were complete, along with all of the pertinent data. Then we would, again as a team, come to a consensus concerning a final recommendation. Of course, I was stuck with the final out-briefing of the hopeful flier.

Of those 540 fliers we saw the first year I was there, we recommended 209 of them be returned to flight status. It was estimated that we had saved the Air Force about seventy-five million dollars, which is what it would have cost to have replaced these men.

Newspaper article highlights money saving "Aeromedical Consultation Service"

It didn't take long before I realized the gold mine of medical data this Service had been gathering over the several years it had been functioning. I started to look at cases by specific disease, comparing data and final outcomes. Over the next two years, I had five articles published in the *"International Journal of Aerospace Medicine"* and several more in Air Force safety magazines. Some of the articles concerned subjects like "Aortic Insufficiency in Fliers" (study of heart-valve disease), "Alternobaric Vertigo," and "Multiple Sclerosis in Fliers." I even wrote one on "Paranoid Schizophrenia in Fliers." Of course, in the articles I never mentioned anything that could identify the pilots, but the data was real and very interesting, as well as educational.

20

~ Too Tall Joe Or Just Don't Close The Hatch ~

In and amongst our Consultation Service patients, my group was tasked with doing some of the medical selections for the Space Program. The Manned Orbiting Lab had been built and crew members had to be selected. Additionally, the Space Program was now open for the selection of a few physicians and scientists as well as for more pilots and crew members. I was doing the medical exams on several of the new candidates and had seriously considered that I might meet all the qualifications for a Scientist Astronaut. Then the medical criteria was published by NASA and I lost out by two inches in height. At that time, I was six-feet-two-inches, but no one over six feet was allowed in the Program because the Gemini (and maybe Apollo) capsule hatch could not be closed if a crew member was taller than six feet. So much for my dreams of being an Astronaut. Maybe the amulet was watching out for me.

I personally wanted to see a physician go up, but as I examined the candidates, one by one they were disqualified. The final physician candidate stepped into my office. Like myself, he was an Aerospace Medical Specialist and all his credentials looked good. He was a Navy guy—but I didn't hold that against him! His name was Joe Kerwin, and when he stepped onto the scale and I measured his height, he was six-feet-and-one-quarter-inches tall! We both looked in disbelief—this couldn't be. He was our last candidate in the current group. I asked Joe to step out of my office and come in again. We would start all over again. Joe smiled at me and nodded. When he returned to my office, his back was curved, his belly was out, and his head was not exactly all the way up. Back on the scale, and glory be—a "miracle!" Joe measured just a fraction under six feet. The rest of his physical was a breeze. To make a long story short, Joe completed astronaut training, and eventually spent thirty days in space in the Manned Orbit Laboratory, where he conducted multiple and important medical experiments.

Weeks after that mission was finished, I was surprised to get a large envelope in the mail. Inside it was a beautiful 8 x 10 colored photo of Joe in his space suit. The inscription is priceless to me, and it reads, *"To Larry, from your grateful 5' 11-7/4" examinee, Joe Kerwin".*

My "thanks" from Joe Kerwin, astronaut

21

~ Puddle Jumping The Pacific ~

In the Spring of 1969, I was promoted to Lt. Colonel and then, later that Fall, assigned as Chief of Aerospace Medicine for all Air Defense Command, country-wide. I was transferred to Colorado Springs, Colorado, to the Air Defense Command Headquarters, working directly for the Command Surgeon who was a Brigadier General. My job included occasional visits inside Cheyenne Mountain to see to the medical condition of the entire hospital built in that facility. My responsibilities also covered monitoring all of the Air Defense Command Flight Surgeon's offices in the U.S. My favorite friend was, again, the Command Safety Officer. We could borrow a T-33 and fly to Minot, North Dakota, in just a few hours (no comments please).

Larry and his T-33

The work was mostly administrative, but I also had a small clinic there at headquarters. In my spare time I wrote several more medical articles, two of which were picked up by the Canadian Air Force Air Defense Group and published in their Safety magazine. Administration is the "dues" one has to pay if you're a manager in, or out of, the Air Force.

A message was sent to all departments at Air Defense headquarters saying that our Three Star Commander of Air Defense Command, and his staff, would be going on a two-week site evaluation mission completely around the Pacific Rim. His purpose was to visit our Air Defense personnel who were supporting some of our allied countries and to inspect our facilities and coordinate efforts with his allied counterparts. So he and his staff would be "out of town" for a couple of weeks. An added note to the Medical Department stated that the General wanted to take his personal Flight Surgeon with him on this tour. You can guess who that was. Commanders of his rank had their own airplanes and his was a four piston-engined C-118, a military version of the civilian Douglas DC-6.

The Douglas DC-6

It was an intercontinental airliner that could carry either about eighty-five people or twelve tons of cargo, or a combination of each. It also had a pressurized cabin so it could fly at 28,000 feet with an inside cabin pressure of about 6,000 feet. It had a range of almost three thousand miles and a speed of about 300 mph. Harry Truman's Presidential aircraft was such a plane. On our trip, we had some fifteen people on board, including the flight crew. I was told to bring my dress uniform along, which meant there could be semi-formal receptions and dinners to attend. Additionally, I packed a good-sized medical kit to cover diseases and illnesses for all occasions. After departing Peterson Field in Colorado Springs, we refueled on the west coast before proceeding to Hawaii. At the risk of making this sound like a travelogue, I do need to relate where we went and the many remarkable people and locations we encountered.

Oahu was a two-day rest stop. Don't ask me what we were "resting" from. I didn't ask the General. Of course, I had to see Duke Kahanamoko's and listen to Don Ho sing "Tiny Bubbles."

Then it was off to Clark Air Force Base in the Philippines. Many of us who were newcomers to that area were disappointed to see how every house and yard near the base had to have high stone or concrete walls, topped with broken glass, to keep the criminals out. We spent only one night there and left early the next morning.

We support a couple of surveillance units in New Zealand. Driving the back roads of that country, we spent more time waiting for herds of sheep to make way for us than we did visiting the sites. But the country was beautiful, especially Christ Church and Wellington, as well as the mountains and cliffs overlooking the seas.

The Australians greeted us like cousins, and they gave a party for us that just about used up my full supply of Alka-Seltzer. We managed to cover Sydney, Melbourne and Adelaide before heading to Alice Springs. Out there, the flies and the 'roos (kangaroos) claimed most of our attention. Our surveillance support team was situated in the Outback on a small mountain. We did make a flight west out over Uluru (once known as Ayer's Rock). That's some big rock! Crocodile Dundee would have been proud of us. Keep in mind that this was also a "goodwill" tour and an "attaboy" for our servicemen stationed there. Certainly gracious hosting and a solidification of our friendships with the Aussies were a necessary part of it. We concluded our five days in Australia's capitol, Canberra. That was pretty sobering.

Our next stop was Taipei. Our General and his staff (including me) each received a personally engraved invitation to have dinner with the Commander-in-Chief of the Chinese Air Force, General Chen I-fan. We were requested to wear business suits, and I noticed that the RSVP on the invitation was crossed out. Choosing not to attend was not an option and no reply was necessary. We would attend!

At the seven-course dinner each guest had a separate attendant serving him. Already on the tables when we sat down were several different foods, most of which I could not identify. I did recognize the consommé soups, served with pigeon eggs floating about. Sheep's brains were a warm side dish served with the main meat course (unknown meat!), and so it went. No one called me that night about any gastrointestinal problems, so I counted my blessings.

We were housed in private rooms at Madame Chiang Kai Sheck's opulent Resort Hotel overlooking the East China Sea. Now, that was how to live! Before we left the next day, a huge and very heavy crate was loaded on board our aircraft. I discovered later that it was a hand-made, hand-carved, huge teak wood desk. A gift from one General to another? I really don't know the answer to that.

In South Korea, we landed at three bases: one near Inchon, one at Taegu, and one at Pusan. Officially, the North/South Korean War had not really ended. Only a truce was in effect; and so, at each base when we landed, we encountered multiple machine gun bunkers and anti-aircraft guns all over the airfield.

A dinner there was somewhat less formal but, fortunately, we were not served Kimshi. Better yet, each member of our

General's staff was presented a beautiful 5 x 7 inch lacquered box with the South Korean Eagle, four stars, and "Republic Of Korean Air Force" inlaid on the cover. Inside the cover was a small plaque which said "Presented by General Kim Too Man, Chief of Staff, ROK Air Force." Yes, I still have it.

At Yakota Air Force Base in Japan, we spent three days. The General had a special invitation to accompany some Japanese generals and dignitaries to a distant resort for the weekend, no other staff members required. So I had the weekend off to tour the area and do some shopping. How can one be gone flying around half of the world and not come home with something for the family? I finally settled on a large box of Noritake China dinner service, a complete setting for eight, for my wife; a 2 x 4 foot electric Pachinko game for the kids; plus, a few small Oriental memorabilia. The General returned to Yakota two days later, none the worse for wear. Now we were off to Alaska after all members of the staff and crew loaded the many boxes and cartons from their shopping sprees (contents unknown to me).

I say Alaska, but the first stop we made heading for the North American mainland had to be the most God-forsaken military station in our property repertoire, Adak. Adak is a tiny island located far out, near the western tip of the Aleutian Islands. If you landed short, or long, you were likely to be in the Bering Sea. No trees existed on the island. It was simply one big rock! The unit there was very small, and in about two hours on the ground, the boss met and saw everyone and everything. This was early Fall, and I wouldn't even want to *think* about spending a winter there!

Anchorage, Alaska, was our overnight, as well as our refueling, stop. What can one buy in Anchorage, you may well ask? How about frozen prawn tails the size of small bananas? Or frozen Alaskan King Crab legs? But how to bring these frozen delicacies back to Colorado Springs without having them thaw out? There were no ice chests on board. What one has to have on trips like this is an ingenious crew chief, a good Master Sergeant.

Our "Chief" met the criteria exactly and rigged some kind of secure places up inside the aircraft's wheel wells. This is the area into which the landing gear retracts, and it was neither pressurized, like the inside of the aircraft, nor heated. At about twenty thousand feet, it made the perfect freezer. Departing Anchorage with its load of people, their baggage, and a great deal of "personal procurements" from various countries, the aircraft was, indeed, "loaded." Additionally, in order to make a non-stop flight from Anchorage to Colorado Springs carrying all that extra weight, we took on every ounce of fuel the tanks could hold. On the take-off roll, it seemed we would never get off the ground, but those four big Pratt & Whitney R 2800 radial engines did their job and got us airborne. All was well for the first thirty minutes until, out over the Gulf of Alaska, one of those engines failed and had to be shut down.

We had to turn back to Anchorage. There is something you should understand about large reciprocating-engined aircraft and fuel. On the ground you can load them up and, with a long enough runway, they are designed to eventually, in spite of the fuel load, get you into the air. But, they are not designed to land with a full load of fuel as the landing gear would never support the weight when it hit ground. The only option then is to offload thousands of pounds of fuel in the air before attempting to land; and that's exactly what we did, streaming the evaporating fuel across the Alaskan Gulf for about twenty minutes. Thirty-six hours later, with a repaired engine, we did the whole take-off bit again. I think we were all happy to complete the mission and to get home.

22

~ Educating A Bird ~

Very early in 1971, much to my great surprise, I was notified of my promotion to full "bird" Colonel, effective January 20. Then, only a few weeks later, came the biggest surprise yet. But let me explain something first. Each year, in all of the Air Force (about 800,000 at that time), a total of 350 Air Force Officers are selected to attend a senior service school. About 220 of those are selected to attend the Air War College. Those who are selected are picked by a board which reviews all the efficiency reports of each potential candidate officer who has already been promoted to full colonel or is pegged for that promotion in the very near future. While there are always exceptions, it is most likely that future generals will come through one of those service schools.

The Air War College is a ten-month course which begins in the summer and ends the following spring. Usually, almost all of the "selectees" are "line" officers. They are mostly pilots, but there are some with technical specialties. After completing the course successfully, each one has the potential to be a future leader.

A top secret clearance is required for those who attend the school. Of the 221 selectees for the Air War College course, beginning in the summer of 1971, one physician was named. Guess who? I was absolutely shocked. I had never even considered that course, I certainly never mentioned it, and there was no such thing as applying for it. Just some folks in a back room chose from your military history and decided who would take the course. The next five months were the slowest I can remember.

In June 1971, I moved into small quarters at Maxwell Air Force Base, Montgomery, Alabama, to attend the Air War College. I had no idea about the detailed nature of the course. I was absolutely NOT about to wage a war or lead any army or air wing.

The course was actually about how the world runs, how governments are run. It was about economics, industries, treaties, international law, and so much more. The class was broken up into small seminar groups of fifteen students per classroom. Most of each day was spent in that classroom, but for several hours each week all 200+ of us were gathered in a large lecture room listening to a speaker of special talent.

Famous correspondent Walter Kronkite spoke to us about the media. A Russian major, who had defected from the KGB, spoke to us about the Soviet Union and its ambitions (1971 version). Top university economists spoke about government expenditures. International legal experts spoke on how treaties and international agreements worked. Yes, we did learn about classified new weapon systems, and we learned about the inside workings of the CIA and the FBI. In my seminar group of fifteen, we had nine Air Force officers, one Army colonel, one RAF wing commander, one CIA agent, an NSA agent, and one FBI agent. We also had an amazing engineer from Lockheed Aircraft Company named Kelly Johnson.

The designer of the U-2, Kelly Johnson (Air War College)

Who is C. L. (Kelly) Johnson? He is the inventor, designer, and builder of the U-2 spy plane; the one Gary Powers flew over Russia and other pilots flew over Cuba photographing the Russian missiles that led to the Cuban Missile Conflict in 1961. What a group of talented people, and what stories we shared, but for our ears only . . . sorry. The whole program was a wake-up call. The bottom line was—*believe very little of what you read in the media, and only half of what you think you see.*

Now being a class, it was tradition that we would have a Class Yearbook by the end of the ten months. Every other class in the past had one. Early on in a seminar, the whole group was asked if anyone had any experience in writing or working on one. While some had a little, I had been the associate editor of my high school yearbook at the Military Academy. The "powers that were" at the time decided that was sufficient experience for the task, and I was elected Editor-in-Chief of the Air War College Yearbook for the Class of 1971. I had a great staff of about ten people, and the book had some terrific pictures and some great stories.

YEARBOOK COMMITTEE

Editor-In-Chief, Larry Enders
Copy Editor, Ted Ladd
Layout Editor, Jack Gentry
Photo Editor, Skip Jones
Business Manager, Bill Brockman

AWC Yearbook Editor-in-Chief and chief advisor

Editorial staff, AWC Yearbook (left to right) Jack Gentry, Ted Ladd, Larry Enders, Skip Jones and Bill Brockman

As part of our studies, we each had to write a thesis on a subject of our choice. I wrote a position paper on the potential benefits of "Establishing a Government-Sponsored Medical School." I didn't win the Commandant's Award for it, but I did get an Honorable Mention. (Actually, I think it was in the men's room that I heard it "mentioned!")

The course opened my eyes to numerous things about which most of us have many misconceptions. For me, it was especially so on the subject of Treaties and International Law. I asked one of our speakers, "But how can a certain nation do this or that? How can one country simply walk across another's border when a Non-Aggression Treaty is in place? Isn't that type of action covered by International Law, signed by all these countries?" He gave me this condescending smile and answered my question before my two hundred classmates, "Treaties are only a piece of paper and so is International Law. Countries sign them when it's in their best interests to sign them, they live by them when it is in their best interests to live by them, and they break them when it's in their best interests to break them. For the most part, that's the way it is, and that's the way it always has been."

How's that for bursting your bubble? And you thought all those things meant something. The whole year was an eye-opener, something not available to the civilian population. It was a new take on how the world of politics works, and it could make one quite cynical.

23

~ Not With *My* Dog! ~

After ten months at Air War College, I was totally out-of-cycle as far as medical assignments go. Except for the Southeast Asia tour, I was being transferred about every two years, so this was going to be a mid-period move for me.

I was assigned the position of Director of Base Medical Services at McChord AFB in the state of Washington. This was an Air Defense Command base located in one of the most scenic areas in our country. The Tacoma-Seattle area is beautiful, with the Puget Sound to the west and the Cascade Mountains and Mt. Rainier to the east. After only one-and-a-half years there, I received a call from the Surgeon General's office in Washington, D.C. Two hospital commander positions were going to be open shortly, and I was being offered a choice. One site was at Hickam Field in Hawaii and the other was in the middle of the Mojave Desert in California. I know what you're thinking—a "no-brainer," right? Not so fast . . . a few more specifics, please.

"Hawaii is a three-year tour at a small hospital on the island and, by the way, we hope you don't have a dog. "There has never been a case of rabies in Hawaii, and if you want to bring a dog with you, it will have to go into cage quarantine for at least one month." *Not my dog!*

The position in The Mojave Desert would be as Commander of a fifty-bed hospital at Edwards AFB, home of the Air Force Flight Test Center and the Air Force Test Pilots' School. Oh, by the way, there was one other point to consider. Normally all physician assignments are initiated solely by the Surgeon General's office in Washington. If there is an opening coming up at a facility, the Surgeon General makes the selection and the doctor is sent to that base to fill the slot—no questions asked by the receiving base.

It seems that the Edwards assignment came about a little differently. The Two Star Line General there wasn't particularly fond of doctor officers, in general, because they tended to be somewhat "un-military," and General Lane, if he was anything, was *very* military. He had "suggested" to the Surgeon General's office that the Edwards hospital needed a new, more cooperative officer who could raise the morale of the sluggish group currently occupying that facility. As Commander of the Flight Test Center, Major General Lane insisted on interviewing any prospect for "his" hospital's commander position and that he then be allowed to select the right man.

I opted for Edwards. As I said, I loved my dog! Also, as beautiful as it is, Hawaii (for me) is a wonderful place to vacation but living there for three years was pretty long, confining, and a very great distance from friends and family on the mainland. According to a former "Island" resident, many dwellers there got "Island Fever," eventually feeling overwhelmed by their seclusion from mainland United States. Also, the cost of living was quite high and some thought there was an excess of the Island's "commercial" setting.

It would have been easy for me to jump on a large military plane and hitch a passenger ride to the Edwards area, but, thinking through it, I contacted my usual "go to" guy, our base safety officer at McChord. After calling the general's office and setting up an appointment for the following week, I arranged for a T-33 to be available. On that day our safety guy and I checked out our T-bird, and in my cleanest (but well-worn) flight suit, I flew down the coast, landing at Edwards about fifteen minutes before my scheduled interview. I just knew that the Base Operations Officer would be calling the general right after we shut down the engine and opened the canopy, to let him know whether I climbed out of the front seat or the back seat. I was in the front seat.

A staff car and driver were waiting for me, and we were at the general's office about three minutes before interview time. At exactly 1 p.m., I was ushered into his office by his secretary. He stayed seated and I snapped to attention, performed a perfect salute, and announced "Sir, Colonel Enders reporting as requested." He looked me over from head to foot, stood up, returned my salute, and said, "Well, you look like a military officer." He offered me a seat and began listing his perception of the elements which were lacking in the current hospital regime. Not as bad as I expected.

Then he asked me a few questions about myself—also, not as bad as I expected. The "interview" had lasted only fifteen minutes when he said, "Well, that's all. I'll be talking to the Surgeon General's office later." That didn't tell me too much. I stood at attention, saluted, departed, and was back home well before dinner. The next day my call from Washington was a very short one, "We'll cut your orders for transfer this week. You'll report to Edwards in six weeks." Just that simple. Upon arrival at Edwards, a house was waiting on "Colonel's Row" only three blocks from the hospital, and I walked back and forth each day unless it was raining. I think that may have happened about one day a year!

At fifty beds, the hospital wasn't huge but it was quite complete. On my staff, there were eighteen doctors and fifty-nine nurses, as well as several enlisted medical technicians. The structure itself had been renovated just a few years previously. What had been an unused patient wing had been turned into the administrative wing. My office, having been a four-bed ward, had its own bathroom and shower. The Airman's barracks were built adjacent to the hospital and had a new tennis court.

Edwards Air Force Base hospital—in the desert

That was great because the hospital's First Sergeant and I played tennis at lunch time, almost daily. That included numerous summer days when the noon temperature was about 110 degrees. The interesting thing about that was, after about forty-five minutes on court, neither one of us had even one drop of perspiration on us, only a thin layer of white powder on our skin. The humidity of about 10% was so low that the instant a molecule of moisture surfaced on the skin, it would evaporate, leaving only a trace of dried salt.

I mentioned that the hospital was quite complete. It had an emergency room, X-ray, labs, physical therapy, three operating rooms, and two delivery rooms. We had three flight surgeons, two internists, general surgeons, OB/GYN specialists, pediatricians, an orthopedic surgeon, and a few general duty physicians.

Each day, I was required to attend the general's staff meeting at 9 a.m. The relatively late time allowed me to get to the hospital at about 7:45 a.m and get briefed on anything notable that may have happened throughout the night. I had a hospital staff car to use, for business purposes only, of course. That got me down base to the general's office just in time for his meeting. Usually General Lane conducted any business with me, either at the staff meeting or, if the conversation was for our ears only, directly after. There was rarely a need for me to be called into his presence at any other time. In view of that, I was quite surprised when the general's secretary called me and asked that my wife and I come to the general's house for dinner the next evening with him and Mrs. Lane. Was I being "canned" after only four weeks on base? Logic said that if it was bad news, he would have had me in his office alone.

Next evening at the Lane home, we had drinks and dinner and everything was very cordial, just mostly getting familiar with each other. Then General Lane said, "You seem to be settling in at the hospital quite well. Actually, Mrs. Lane has something she wants to discuss with you." Here's the gist of it. Out there, isolated in the desert, just about everyone lived on the base. We were one great big family. Now, fliers are required to have an annual physical examination, done by a Flight Surgeon. Most of the other military members had scheduled physicals every few years, but the wives on base had no access to a general physical examination unless they become ill or had a medical appointment for a particular problem. Mrs. Lane wanted to know if I had any ideas about how we could remedy that. There were probably five hundred women on the base. I asked if I could get back to her in a couple of days, through the general, and she nodded and dropped the subject. Overall, it was a pleasant evening.

Next day I got together with my hospital administrator and by the following day we had worked out a plan to accomplish the task. At my next meeting with the medical and nursing staff, I laid out our suggestions. Everyone had to be "on board" for it to work—and they were. We were going to "go for it." It was most heartily supported by the nurses who had heard the complaint many times before. The following day, at the general's staff meeting, I presented our suggestion.

"General, if we have your approval, as a spokesmen for the rest of the base, here's how we plan to do it. We're going to completely shut down the hospital for three days, with the exception of the emergency room and emergency surgery. First, we will ask every woman on the base who wishes to have a general physical examination to sign up for one of those three days. We will divide each day's patients into six groups and for specific times. Each queue will line up in a different hallway in the Hospital. There will be six physicians, regardless of his specialties, including myself, doing general physical examinations. Along with the physical, each examinee will have an electrocardiogram and a complete blood count. Depending on findings by the first examiners, the patient may get an X-ray or a pelvic exam by an OB/GYN specialist. In short, everyone will undergo a thorough physical examination and, depending on the findings along the way, further evaluations."

There were many more details, but the bottom line was that each physician examined three patients an hour over a seven-hour period, totalling just under one hundred and thirty a day. At the end of the three days, we had examined, to their satisfaction, almost four hundred ladies, all who had signed up. The hospital staff was proud, the base was proud, and the general was proud (as was Mrs. General).

24

~ A Smash With M*A*S*H ~

There were many happy days in the desert. Because we were relatively isolated, it was quite incumbent upon the residents of our sprawling community to see to their own entertainment. Yes, there were swimming pools, a golf course, tennis courts, and a bowling ally. For larger social gatherings, there was the Officer's Club, NCO Club, and Airman's Club. Well before my arrival at Edwards, there was a custom that every three months one of the tenant organizations had to put on a "theme party" at the Officer's Club and invite all the other organizations. The Base Operations group had put on a "50's Party" and the Test Pilot's School had staged a "Love-In Party," with mattresses scattered all over the floor of the club. Now it was the hospital's turn, and we had to come up with something spectacular.

About this time the "M*A*S*H" television show was very popular, so we decided to go with a "M*A*S*H Party." But it had to be *really* special. One gets to know a lot of people, especially at an isolated base; and some of the associations could be a great help in time of need. So, my first step was to contact some people to ask them for help in planning this really special event.

I required two helicopters to be parked at the front entrance of the "O" Club. Also, we needed a long, large tent to cover the entry walk to the Club's front door—with a big red cross on it and maybe a jeep or two parked near the choppers. We already had enough IV stands and IV bottles (medically for the intake of intravenous fluids) to hang from the stands, complete with tubing fitted with stop/go clips attached. The big surprise was that, unlike a real MASH unit, **our** IV bottles contained Martinis and Margaritas!

But that still wasn't enough. Our hospital administrator and I had an idea. Anyone who watched the TV show always saw the introductory credits naming the producer and director. The director was Gene Reynolds, and we wondered if it would be possible to contact him. Nothing ventured, nothing gained.

My administrator's astute searching came up with his telephone number in Hollywood, which was about one hundred and fifty miles away. I dialed, reached a secretary, and, after explaining the reason for my call, was actually put through to Gene Reynolds himself! Small miracles sometimes still happen. I explained to him who I was, where I was, and the hospital's quest to come up with the best "M*A*S*H Party" yet. Then I popped the question, "Mr. Reynolds, is it possible to have a member of the cast attend our party?" There was silence for a minute, then he quietly said, "Okay, Doc. I'll look into it and get back to you in a few days." I thanked him and ended the call. The next day I said to my administrator, "I believe we've heard the last from Mr. Reynolds."

Two days later my phone rang. I answered, and the voice said, "Hi, Doc. Gene Reynolds here. I looked into your request and here's the situation." I was expecting a very short "sorry" and a hang up, but that's not what happened. He continued, "As you know, we are at our taping hiatus for the summer. Alan Alda is in Europe on another project, but Jamie Farr ("Klinger") and Bill Christopher ("Father Mulcahy") and Bill's wife, Barbara, would be happy to attend." For a moment, I couldn't believe my ears.

Reynolds continued, "But here's the deal. You'll have to provide the transportation back and forth from their homes to your party." Without knowing if I could deliver or not, I said, "No problem." Reynolds then said, "And there's another thing—that's a long ride out there, and both Jamie and Bill like Scotch. I highly recommend that in the back seat of your car you have an ice bucket and a bottle of good Scotch." He then gave me the home address of Jamie Farr in Tarzana (Los Angeles) and said he'd arrange for the Christophers to be at Farr's house at 5 p.m. on party night. Even though I thanked him profusely, I still couldn't believe my ears.

The prerequisites of Mr. Reynolds presented a few small problems. I did have a hospital staff car so I could handle the transportation part, even though it wasn't going to be exactly for business. Bending the rules a little more was having an open bottle of Scotch in a Government vehicle. That's a big "no-no." Well, sometimes in life one must learn to improvise. The Scotch would be "medicinal" if it was used to calm the passengers in the car; and the car itself was to be used to transport "Dignitaries to a Military Function" established for the morale of the troops. Sounded good to me!

In a few days I checked again with Gene Reynolds to confirm that this was, indeed, going to happen. He told me it was, and then we began sending invitations to all organizations on the base, advertising that Klinger and Father Mulcahy would be attending. Almost everyone I talked to before the party was assuming that somebody on the hospital staff would be impersonating Klinger and Father Mulcahy. We had no comment about this other than, "Whatever!"

On the day of the big party, I drove the staff car myself rather than have a driver, especially with the Scotch and the large bucket of ice in the back. We also had plastic "glasses" and some napkins available. I prayed I would not be involved in an accident, and headed for Tarzana, map in hand, at about two-thirty in the afternoon.

Jamie Farr (Klinger) from the TV series M*A*S*H

Arriving at Jamie Farr's house, I saw him there with Bill and Barbara Christopher. The Farrs were having a new pool installed in their side yard. Mrs. Farr was overseeing the work and would not be going with us. After introductions all around, we piled into the staff car and headed out to the base. Barbara Christopher was about six months pregnant, so I guaranteed all on board that she would not be thrown into the Club pool that night. Jamie Farr needed the same guarantee, but not Bill Christopher. So, before the night was over, he took a very good-hearted dunking.

Jamie Farr, Barbara and Bill Christopher (Fr. Mulcahy of M*A*S*H*)

Fr. Mulcahy (Bill Christopher) gets dunked in the pool

We arrived back at the base early enough to stop at my house for a preliminary libation, although I'm not sure that was necessary because Jamie and Bill had helped themselves generously to the "provisions" in the back seat—all the way out from LA. Barbara had passed on the refreshments but did appreciate the "rest stop" at my home. We relaxed a bit and then proceeded to the club.

There was an "announcer" at the club using a microphone to herald the arrival of our special guests. About two hundred and fifty people were in attendance, and they all stopped and waited to see the "impersonators" arrive. When they saw the real Klinger and Fr. Mulcahy come in, they were stunned. From there on, the party was fabulous. The General and the other ten commanders met our guests, who were, of course, the "hits" of the party. Bill Christopher was thrown into the pool by several of our nurses dressed in bikinis, and he seemed to have no major objections to that. We have a photo of him, standing waste deep in the pool, holding up his two-fingered "V "as he often did on the TV show. I guess I wasn't too surprised when the next victim for the pool was me.

Barbara Christopher was a sweetheart and went along with everything. About 2 a.m. I had our hospital driver take our guests back home to the LA area. Needless to say, that party was the talk of the base for weeks. The General congratulated me and the whole hospital staff for the diligent work involved in hosting such a unique affair. The entire staff made points for their efforts.

25

~ A Hole In My Heart ~

But not all days were happy days in the desert. There were also some very unhappy times. One of our major missions at Edwards was the flight testing of new, experimental aircraft or new systems being tested in aircraft currently in use. In time, I met and befriended many of the test pilots.

As I said earlier, I played tennis several days a week during the lunch hour, mostly with our First Sergeant. Periodically, however, he was unable to play due to some other commitments; and on those days, I would drive further to our other tennis courts on the base. There was almost always someone playing, and I would be invited to join them. It was there that I met Mike and Betty Love. Mike was a test pilot, and both were just great people. They were in their early 30's and obviously very much in love. Every now and then Mike would come alone to play, or sometimes Betty would come alone. I would always play with one or the other. We did this for about one year.

On a base whose primary mission is testing, there are, on occasion, going to be mishaps. When an aircraft accident did occur, it was usually in the vicinity of the huge base, and the word spread almost instantaneously. If a test pilot did not survive the crash, there was a "notification ritual" which, to me, seemed a bit awkward. The center commander, the hospital commander, and the chief chaplain were notified immediately and would meet at some designated location. Then all three would get into the general's car and proceed to the home of the deceased flier to jointly notify the wife and/or family.

On a particularly blue-skied morning at about 10 a.m., a test pilot took off in a modified F-4 Fighter Bomber. This particular aircraft was a tried and true combat plane, one of the mainstays of the Vietnamese conflict. Something went wrong on take-off. The aircraft lost power and a fire developed in the cockpit. Protocol called for the pilot to eject immediately, but, as I understand it, the fire was in an area under the pilot's seat and it disabled the ejection mechanism. He was trapped in the F-4 and, as a result, went into the ground with his plane. As you've probably guessed, the pilot was my friend, Mike Love.

General Stafford picked me up at the hospital; we then picked up the chaplain and headed for Mike and Betty's house on base. Pilots' wives have a second sense about some things, and their husband's safety is high on that list. The explosion and the crash could be heard over most of the base, and Betty knew the time of Mike's test flight for that morning. The front door of their house had a small glass window in the upper part. As we drove up to the house, we could see Betty's face looking out at us. Even if her instincts hadn't been working, just seeing the general's car pulling up in her driveway at ten in the morning, carrying the general, the doctor, and the chaplain, was an undeniable giveaway.

Betty watched as we walked up to the door. I was the only one who knew her personally. She looked at me, put her hands over her face, and we heard the door being locked. She walked away. We rang, we knocked, I called her name, but she never did let us in. A friend of hers, the wife of another test pilot, pulled up. She knew and said Betty would let her in after a while and we could leave. We did. I saw Betty a couple of times after that fateful day. One day she came to the hospital to thank me for being a friend to both Mike and her, and she gave me a big hug. Two weeks later, Betty moved from the base. The day of that crash was one of the *worst days* of my service career.

26

~ Doc-In-Demand ~

There were always changes going on in the service. General Lane had received his third star (Lieutenant General) and had been transferred to the biggest base (area-wise) in the Air Force. He was now the commander at Eglin AFB in Fort Walton Beach, Florida, the home of the Armament Development Center. Edwards, the second largest base (area-wise) tested newly developed aircraft, for the most part. When the Air Force wants a newer, faster, technologically superior fighter bomber, the civilian contractors all come up with their designs and the bidding starts. When it comes down to the final one or two, the prototypes go to Edwards where the test pilots put them through their paces to see if they really can perform as the contractor said they could.

Once a plane has been tentatively selected, it is sent to Eglin. A new, fast, great aircraft is no good just by itself—it must be fitted with armament. Guns, cannons, rockets, bomb racks are added, and then it is flown again to see if it still performs as promised. When the munitions are fired or dropped, accuracy is assessed as well as the plane's performance during the "live firing" exercise. Eglin AFB is big because it has the live weapon ranges where the firing and detonations can be held without fear of endangering the public. Eglin had several other large units located there, including the Eglin AFB Hospital, a 210-bed Regional Medical Referral Center. It had every specialty there was and received patients from the entire eastern coast of the United States.

Back at Edwards, my new boss was none other than Major General Tom Stafford, former astronaut and a four space flight veteran. Tom had been on the Gemini VI and Gemini IX missions; both of which I worked. Later, he made a flight to the moon to select a landing site for the lunar excursion module. He was also commander of the first American/Russian Space Flight called the Apollo/Soyuz. Now he had returned to the Air Force and, having been a test pilot himself, was the new Commander at the Flight Test Center. Tom was my neighbor living just two houses from me. It was good to see him again, and he was happy to see me.

All was well in the desert.

It was only about seven or eight months after General Stafford's arrival, in April of 1976 if my memory serves me well, that I received another call from the Surgeon General's office in Washington. It seemed that General Lane had just "excused" the medical commander of the Regional Hospital at Eglin, and he was requesting me to replace him. Going from a 50-bed base hospital to a 210-bed Regional Medical Center was quite a jump!

Larry and General Tom Stafford

I wasn't worried about doing the job. However, I was concerned that I would not be too popular with other Air Force hospital commanders who would normally be in line for such a promotion because they had been in charge of much larger hospitals than I had. But, I also couldn't turn the job down. Additionally, if the Air Force Surgeon General didn't think I could handle it, he would have said that to General Lane.

Eglin Air Force Base Regional Medical Center (210 beds)

27

~ "Dining In" / "Dining Out" ~

I arrived at Eglin in the summer and set up housekeeping in a very comfortable home on the base, reserved for the Hospital Commander. I discovered that I had an outstanding exec as my administrator. He kept the hospital administration working like clockwork. It made me wonder why the previous commander had been ushered out.

It took me several weeks to figure it out. With about eighty-five doctors, twice as many nurses, several medical admins, plus a large group of corpsmen, the medicine being practiced there was quite good. The problem was, there was no unity. The hospital personnel did not work together as a team and had no team spirit. They came to work each day, did their work, and then left at the end of the day. As General Lane said to me, "No Esprit de Corps."

Many of the doctors were two-year men and felt no allegiance to their organization; they just wanted to put in their time and then go home. Even some of the regular officers were listless. This is the type of problem that General Lane blames on lack of good leadership. The staff didn't really know their previous commander and had no particular respect for him, other than that he had "Eagles" on his shoulders.

My administrator and I put our heads together and came up with a few ideas that could hopefully improve the current attitude. The first idea, when it was announced, went over like the proverbial "lead balloon." I ordered that on a certain date, in about one month's time, we would have a formal "Dining In." What is a "Dining In," you ask? A "Dining In" is a military formation which requires all officers under one's command to don his or her formal Mess Dress uniform and attend a lengthy dinner with a lot of formalities. It actually began in England and is a very old tradition. Early on it was a custom in monasteries and was then taken up by the universities and spread to the military. At a "Dining In" the commanders of all the other units on base are invited as guests. The chaplain begins with a benediction, and sometime during the night a guest speaker lays on a talk of around forty-five minutes. Sounds pretty boring, doesn't it?

The grumbling amongst the troops, especially the young two-year doctors, was unavoidable. When young doctors or nurses enter the service, they are given a clothing allowance to buy their uniforms and a list telling them what they would need; summer pants and shirts, winter pants and shirts, a blouse, ties, caps, and insignia. Also listed is a Mess Dress uniform, the cost of which was (then) about $150. The amount of money they were given was about $600 to $650. But word gets around that buying the Mess Dress is probably not necessary, as some medical folks go through their whole two years and never have occasion to use it. It's like buying a tux in the civilian world. So most of the young people simply skip buying the Mess Dress, hoping it'll never be called for, and pocket the extra money. And now, this new idiot hospital commander says they need it!

Eight of the two-year doctors actually unified and asked for a meeting with General Lane to protest their being pushed to participate in this "Dining In." They wanted to skip the dinner and, therefore, the need to fork out the $150. On meeting with General Lane, their position was, "We don't want to go to this dinner and, therefore, we shouldn't have to buy a Mess Dress Uniform, Sir." General Lane calmly stood up and replied, "Gentlemen, hear me loud and clear. Any commander's call for a "Dining In" is not an RSVP request; it is a mandatory military formation. And unless you're all prepared to be court-martialed, *you will attend*. This meeting is ended." Good man, that General Lane.

The preparations for the Mess proceeded. There's a lot more I haven't explained. At the head table, which was on a dais, would be the President of the Mess (that would be me) along with all the guest commanders, the speaker, and the chaplain. At the farthest-most table across from the dais, and set for one, would be "Mister Vice." If any attendee had a comment to make or wanted to make a toast, he or she would have to stand and be recognized by Mister Vice before they could speak.

Mister Vice was appointed to that position by the President of the Mess and was, traditionally, the youngest and lowest-ranked officer in the organization. So, for our "Dining In," it was Miss Vice, one of our newer nurses. She was well briefed on her duties, which were steeped with tradition. As the attendees gathered, smoking was allowed. The "Smoking Lamp," which was situated at the head table for all to see, was lit. At the ringing of a bell, everyone went to their tables, and usually at this time the "Smoking Lamp" was extinguished.

There was another relatively small table just in front of the head table. On this table was a very large punch bowl with a bilious green liquid, generously laced with clear ethyl alcohol. There were wine glasses at each place setting, as toasting was always first on the list at these functions. The "grog bowl" (the green stuff) was the "penalty bowl" for infraction of any military specifications brought to the attention of the President by any other attendee. Of course, this was a farce and contrived.

Starting with the smoking lamp being extinguished, the President of the Mess stands and announces that the Mess is called to order. He then calls for the chaplain to give benediction, which is usually "short and sweet." He then introduces the guests at the head table, with the exception of the speaker (that would come later). Following the introductions, the President raises his glass, asks for all to stand, and orders a toast to the Commander-in-Chief, to which they all reply "To the President" and down the first glass of wine. Then the "toasting" begins in earnest. Waiters stand by with extra bottles of wine to refill any empty glass. "To the Chief of Staff of the Air Force." "To the Secretary of Defense." "To the Governor of the State," and so on. It goes on for quite a while (too many dignitaries, so little wine, right?).

Following the toasts from the dais, any attendee was allowed to be recognized by Miss Vice and could then propose a toast. This continues on for some time until the President of the Mess calls it to an end. By this time the mess "inmates" seemed to have brightened up a bit. Things were not quite as "stuffy" as they thought it would be.

The Grog Bowl plays a big part in the festivities. It begins with one of the veteran officers asking to be recognized. After recognition has been given, the officer states (as an example), "Captain So-and-So seems to have a bottom button on his blouse unfastened, and it is requested that he be directed to report to the Grog Bowl." The Captain in question must go to the Grog Bowl, draw a dipper full of the brew, fill a glass, and then down the liquid, while everyone applauds. The crowd caught on quite quickly, and soon everyone was consumed with finding an insignia a half-inch off center, a tie not straight, or some other trivial thing. It didn't make any difference because, very soon, there were smiles all 'round. The meal was always grand and well worth the "fare," which, by the way, was zero for those in attendance. It was "on the hospital."

Before dessert, a break of about fifteen minutes was called and the smoking lamp was again lit. The bell signaled "reassemble" and dessert was served. The time had come for me to introduce the speaker. He was there as a favor to me. All the attendees were stunned when I presented "Major General and Astronaut, Thomas Stafford—four-time space flier, including a trip to the moon." I doubt any of the hospital staff had ever even seen an astronaut in person before and certainly never up this close talking directly to them.

Larry introduces General Tom Stafford at Dining In

They all stood and cheered as Tom took the microphone. I had briefed General Stafford on the reluctance of some concerning the Mess, and he fixed that from the very beginning. When the applause died down, he asked me to stand with him. He put his arm around my shoulder and then told the audience how honored he was when I called asking him to be the speaker in front of so many doctors and nurses. Then he went on to say how the astronauts would never have gotten to the moon without the medical support from guys like me and how much he appreciated it. He took my hand and thanked me profusely.

Well, my status with the hospital staff jumped about a thousand per cent after that. Down the table, General Lane gave me a thumbs up and smiled. This was as good as it gets. Bottom line? The "Dining In" was a great success. The eight dissident doctors showed up at the general's office two days later to apologize for their previous behavior. They also told him that they had never had a better time. They had never come to me before the event, so they didn't come to me after it, but the hospital group came together more like a unit and we had a team going again. All's well that ends well.

Things were going fairly well at the hospital, but this was no time to rest on our laurels. About six months after the well received "Dining In," we had another idea. Wives were frequently being left out of military events. But there was a cure for that, a "Dining Out." What is a "Dining Out," you ask? It's a "Dining In" but with wives/partners included. The protocol was the same. All the various unit commanders on the base, with wives/partners, were invited. It was still going to be relatively formal, Mess Dress for the military members, formal gowns for the ladies. Every wife jumped at the idea—finally a reason to really dress up! The hospital wives spread the word like the wind, and the date was set.

I had the same dilemma as before, who to ask as the guest speaker? It had to be somebody "big" to match Tom Stafford's presentation. The old "give it a shot" feeling was stirring again. Why not? Who is the very, very top guy in the Air Force who knew his stuff about medical people and the turmoil their wives have to go through, following their husbands around the world? The Surgeon General of the whole Air Force, that's who!

In this case it was Lt. General (Three Star) George Shafer. Did General Shafer and I have any kind of relationship between us? In a way, yes, we did. He was a colonel when he ran the Aerospace Medical Residency Program, and I and my nine friends were his students. He was our mentor for those three years. A few years later he became the Commander of the School of Aerospace Medicine and during that tenure was promoted to Brigadier General. He was also the one who caught me flying all those combat missions in Southeast Asia and made me stop. In view of all that, would he consent to fly down from Washington to Florida just to speak at my "Dining Out"? You bet your life he would, and he did!

***Lt. Gen. George Shafer (Air Force Surgeon General)
speaks at Dining Out***

His first-hand knowledge of the trials and tribulations that came with being a military medical doctor, and having a military wife who had to keep that "stiff upper lip" so often, enthralled the crowd. During his address, husbands cheered and wives cried. Of course, the Grog Bowl was active, as usual, and added to the intimacy between the speaker and his audience. General George was even invited to "partake of the Bowl" because this was a "Dining Out" and he had failed to bring his wife. I think he had a double dip! The hospital had hit another home run!

As the months went by, the hospital outpatient clinics were enlarged to accommodate more patients. In the Fall, the Medical Inspector General's team from Washington came to give the facility a thorough examination. These evaluations were done periodically at all Air Force hospitals to ensure that the facility was operating safely, efficiently, and in compliance with Air Force Regulations. They also checked on the quality of patient care and patient satisfaction. We did quite well with very few items upon which we needed to improve. I was asked periodically to augment this inspection team and to examine other large hospitals throughout the country.

One of my personal peculiarities as a hospital commander was to leave my office at random times and just browse the facility. It was my belief that there was more to running a hospital than just sitting behind a desk. I would wander about in the patient wards, scan a few charts, and saunter into some of the patients' rooms. There, I would casually ask the patients about how they were doing, were they being treated well, were they satisfied with the service, and so on. I never said who I was, and very few asked me, but they appreciated my concern for their welfare. And some even thanked me for coming by.

After a couple of months of doing this, following the general's staff meeting one morning, he pulled me aside and asked if we had a new chaplain at the hospital. I answered, "No, sir. Why do you ask?" He said that a couple of military wives, at a Wives Club meeting, had mentioned to Mrs. Lane that "this nice man," who they thought must be the chaplain, "had visited them in their hospital rooms." They really appreciated his concern for their welfare, but he never mentioned his position at the hospital." I told the general that it was probably me.

I hadn't told the patients that I was the hospital commander because I wanted their honest opinions about their treatment. General Lane smiled and said, "I knew there was a reason I brought you down here." I have been accused of being many, many things in my life, but, until that moment, never of being a chaplain!

Eglin Air Force Base, Florida

Emergency Room

The Emergency Room is located in the rear of the new wing and is for just that – EMERGENCIES! One of this section's biggest problems is the people that believe they'll get faster service if they wait until after clinic hours and go to the Emergency Room. Not necessarily ture. If you have a minor problem and an emergency comes in - you wait. Everyone is eventually seen, with the more acute seen first.

Emergency Room service is provided around the clock so, if you have a need, call 885-3227. The Hospital recommends asking yourself this question when determining if emergency care is necessary. "Would I be willing to pay a civilian physician to examine me?" If your answer is yes, then go to the Emergency Room. If not, your problem can probably wait until the next day, when you can contact one of the clinics.

Col. Lawrence Enders

Col. Lawrence J. Enders, Commander of the USAF Regional Hospital, at Eglin, is the driving force behind the "open communication concept" now being practiced by the Hospital. Col. Enders assumed command of the Hospital last September and has initiated many new programs to improve not only Hospital conditions but patient, physican relations. (A.A.)

Hospital Commander at work

28

~ Generals & Germans & G-Men, Oh My! ~

In October 1977, I was selected as a military consultant to the Air Force Surgeon General in the specialty of Aerospace Medicine. Fortunately, that didn't involve a move, but it seemed that the "rolling stone" syndrome could not be avoided. Late in the Spring of 1978, I was chosen by the Surgeon General to be the new Commander of the Air Force School of Aerospace Medicine. That certainly was familiar territory. I was going back to Brooks AFB, San Antonio, Texas, for the fourth time. And this time as the Boss!

The job was akin to being the President of a middle-sized university. There was a reasonably large campus with about 16 or 17 separate buildings with almost a thousand people assigned there, mostly military, but with a fairly large contingent of civil service members. The current annual budget was about forty million dollars, and to top it all off, the commander's slot was approved by Congress to be a brigadier general's billet. Most school commanders went there as full colonels. If they performed well for a couple of years, a promotion to brigadier general was usually in order. I was to replace the current brigadier general. To the delight of old friends and neighbors, the San Antonio Express newspaper headlined with a photo, of course, "Enders to head AFB Medical School."

Brooks (SAM) gets a new Chief

Another article, again with photo, "Brooks gets new Chief." My new command contained ten divisions: Education Division, Clinical Sciences, Advanced Development Programs, Crew Technology, Epidemiology, Data Sciences, Hyperbaric Medicine, Radiation Sciences, Technical Services and Veterinary Services. On my previous tours at the school, I had spent most of my time in the Education Division and the Clinical Sciences Division, but I was well acquainted with the other groups and their personnel.

We moved to Brooks in early Summer of 1978. A designated house was waiting for me. The only slightly negative event was my mandatory relief from flying status. It seemed, as an economic move by the Federal Budget Department, all service fliers who had over twenty years of air time were removed from flying status. So much for the $300 a month flight pay. On the other hand, gone were the requirements to get those "harder to acquire" flights, like night time and weather time. Immediately after my arrival there, the departing commander and I, before about a thousand people, went through the formal ceremony of "Change of Command" with me receiving the Commander's Flag.

And then it was time for work. Actually, the first few months were my time for learning. My administrator was a very sharp Civil Service GS-15. By having a permanent GS person in that position, it assured continuity of management and services, even though the medical commanders were rotated every several years. Billy (my administrator) kept a sharp eye on the budget and the physical needs of the multiple buildings and equipment while I tended to the programs, research, and educational duties.

My first personal project was to call in each division leader and receive a thorough briefing on what had been going on, what was going on, and what future projects were anticipated or "hoped for." I was familiar with many of the staff through my previous associations with the SAM. However, there was one person with whom I had little contact during my previous tours, my Chief Scientist, Dr. Hubertus Strughold.

Larry with his Chief Scientist, Dr. Hubertus Strughold

Dr. Strughold was born in Westphalia, Germany, in 1897. He received his doctorate from Göttingen in 1922. He held both an MD and a PhD. His knowledge in the field of Aerospace Medicine allowed him to author several textbooks and more than 180 papers. He was known worldwide as the "Father of Aerospace Medicine." Immediately after World War II, the U.S., England, France, and Russia each scooped up as many German scientists as they could find or steal who might be able to contribute to their country's respective space programs.

Under the CIA's "Project Paperclip," we acquired Dr. Strughold and brought him to the United States. Here, he was installed as the Director of the Department of Space Medicine at the old School of Aviation Medicine at Randolph AFB, Texas. He had written more books there, and was subsequently moved to the new School of Aerospace Medicine at Brooks AFB, Texas, in 1958. There is no question that Dr. Strughold's knowledge of aviation medicine and physiology played an extremely important role in the development of the space suits worn by our astronauts for both orbital and lunar flights.

In 1977, just one year before my arrival, Dr. Strughold was honored when the large Aerospace Medical Library on the SAM campus had its name changed to the Hubertus Strughold Aerospace Medical Library. And now he was Chief Scientist.

COMPENDIUM OF AEROSPACE MEDICINE

VOLUME 2

Hubertus Strughold, M.D., Ph.D.

To School Commander
Col. Lawrence J. Enders
with kind regards & many thanks
Hubertus Strughold

Published January 1979

USAF School of Aerospace Medicine
Aerospace Medical Division (AFSC)
Brooks Air Force Base, Texas 78235

Inside cover page of Dr. Strughold's
Compendium of Aerospace Medicine, Vol. II

But the years had taken their toll on Dr. Strughold and, at age eighty, he spent most of his time writing new books and finishing two previously unpublished Compendiums of Aerospace Medicine—Volume I and Volume II. I was honored when he not only presented me with the two volumes, but had asked me to write the preface in Volume II. Inside the covers of each is written *"To the School Commander, Col. Lawrence J. Enders, with kind regards and many thanks, Hubertus Strughold."*

Hubertus was a bachelor now, his wife having passed away some years before. Within a short time after my arrival, he had developed a practice of dropping into my office unexpectedly about once a week. There seemed to be no purpose to these visits except that he was undoubtedly a very lonesome man. He needed to have someone with whom he could spend some time, and depending upon my schedule, I always gave him as much as I could. He appreciated that. On one of his visits, after a couple of months of just dropping by, he brought to me what he called "a little gift." The gift was a quite old, framed photo of the first ever X-ray. Dr. Strughold told me he had received it at Wurtzburg University in Germany, where he knew Dr. W. C. Roentgen, the man who had discovered the X-ray (then called Bremsstrahluen Rays) in November, 1895.

This picture (X-ray) was of a left hand with two rings on the third finger, indicating that, at that time, scientists did not realize that metal should not be worn during the process. The caption under the picture reads*: "Hand des (unreadable) Geheimrath von Kolliker. Im Physikalischen Institut der Universatat Wurzburg mit X-Strahlen aufgenommen von Professor Dr. W. C. Roentgen."* My best interpretation of this caption says: "The hand of unknown (secret) one from Kolliker in the Physiological Institute of Wurtzburg University using X-Strahlen (rays) and made by Professor W. C. Roentgen."

On another visit from Dr. Strughold, he told me he had something very nice he wanted me to have. Encased in a transparent plastic box, cradled in a styrofoam cushion, was a black, teardrop-shaped rock covered with pock-marked indentations on its surface. Dr. Strughold told me it was a "moon rock." He had been very close to the earlier astronauts who had given him numerous gifts and memorabilia. I asked no questions. He explained that the shape and surface of the rock resulted from meteors hitting the moon, heating the impacted rock to a molten liquid state which then formed a teardrop shape as they "flew away" from the impact area. In their aerial transit they cooled, and the bubble-like pock marks formed as the molten rock solidified. I had no idea if everything he was telling me was true, but it all sounded reasonable. However, I did ask him why he was giving it to me. He looked very sad as he told me, "Because you are a very kind man." Today I keep it in a special, secure place next to a pen Tom Stafford gave me, engraved with his name and which made a transit to the moon with him.

Dr. Strughold made many more trips to my office in those last two years. He talked a little about the past and the difficulty of raising two small children in war-torn Germany but almost nothing about his personal life.

29

~ More Vodka, Please! ~

One would think that by now I would have had my fill of "serendipitous" events; but, actually, the most unusual was still to come. In order for physicians to maintain their license to practice and to continue to be certified in their specialty, they must garner a certain number of "Continuing Medical Education (CME) credits" each year. There are many ways to acquire these credits. Probably the easiest, and least inconvenient for one's working schedule, is to go to a specialty convention. For about five or six days one attends seminars, lectures, and presentations which usually cover the newest advances in your field. For me, each year I attended the International Aerospace Medical Convention. This was usually held in the United States, rotating at one of about a dozen major cities.

In May of 1979, the convention was being held in Washington DC. Conventions of this type served many purposes for the attendees. Not only did they get in their CME's, but they were able to socialize with old friends and associates from other military bases and other countries. Many doctors from foreign countries also attended. There were programs for all the disciplines: doctors, flight nurses, and aeromedical technicians. The entire convention program was usually held in a large hotel with rooms to accommodate evening social functions, award dinners, special group luncheons, and, of course, the educational lectures, and presentations. Also, there was always a very large hall for exhibitors. These exhibitors might be drug companies, airlines, aircraft industries, or displays from foreign countries. I attended this convention, flying there with several other doctors from SAM who were also getting their CME. Since the Air Force was paying for my trip, I was obliged to wear my uniform at all official convention functions. There were uniforms everywhere.

On the last day I was between presentations and chose to browse some of the exhibits. One of the smaller booths that I was walking past was sponsored by the Soviet Union. This was in 1979 and it was still the USSR. It displayed no special items, yet it was "manned" by three gentlemen. One stood just behind the counter which separated him from the convention attendees. The other two stood at the back of the booth with their arms crossed. All were dressed in civilian suits, and I guessed their ages to be in the early thirties. As required, my name tag was pinned to my blouse, last name only. I slowed a bit, looking for some purpose for the booth's existence.

About this time, the gentleman behind the counter said to me, in only slightly-broken English, "Ah, Doctor Enders, how are things going at the School"? I knew I had never met this man before, so I asked, "I'm sorry, but do we know each other?" He smiled and said, "No, but we know you." He put his hand out, which I shook. "And who are you?" I asked. "My name is Leonid Zukov," he said. Nodding towards his two associates he added, "And these gentlemen are Mr. Andrey Zelnikov and Mr. Vladimir Kruzovkin." He then asked me what was new at the School of Aerospace Medicine and what were we doing. Then followed more polite and social conversation. I gave him the information that anyone could find by reading the San Antonio newspaper. I then asked if he was a physician, and he said he was. I asked, "And these gentlemen, also?" nodding toward his two associates. "No, no. And they do not speak English," he replied.

Then he asked if I would do him a favor. Would I consent to him taking photographs of me with him and his associates? After I told him we could do that, he suggested we go outside the hotel into the sunlight for a better picture. The four of us walked out through the front lobby of the hotel, leaving his booth totally unattended. We stopped in the front drive-up area where the light was good. There he took several photos of me with Mr. Zelnikov and Mr. Kruzovkin. Then he took one more. This time the photo included a USAF flight nurse who seemed to appear from nowhere. This was followed by a final photo with Zukov. I recognized the nurse from previous conventions and was pretty certain she did not speak Russian. I asked Zukov why the nurse was in the picture with us. He then explained that because Zelnikov had a dinner date with her for that evening, he had included her as a courtesy. She left the area shortly after, so she and I shared no conversation at all.

Back at the booth, Zukov thanked me for allowing the pictures, then told me that he wanted to give me some memorabilia gifts of our meeting. From below the counter where he stood, he produced a box which contained about ten very unique

Serendipity, the KGB and me

commemorative pins from several different Russian space missions; some of them from the very early Sputnik flights. I believe the pins to be very valuable collectors' items which few Americans would have.

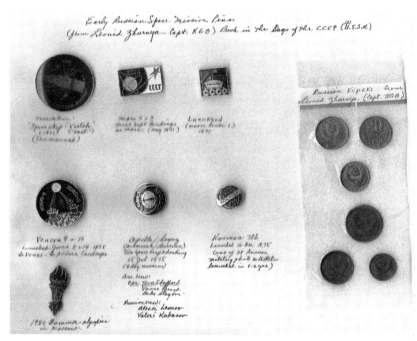

Pins and coins from Leonid

I thanked him, then asked if I would be able to get copies of the photos he had taken. He hesitated for a moment and then gave a vigorously replied, "Yes, of course." I said, "Good. Now, where will you send them?" That prompted him to ask for my full mailing address at the School, naturally. "And how can I contact you?" I asked. "I'd like your address, too." He took a small piece of notepaper and wrote all their names and addresses in both English and Russian. According to that note, he was from the "Institute of Biomedical Problems" in Moscow, on Choroshevskaye Shosse. The other two were from the USSR Academy of Science—Foreign Relations Department. It then struck me as odd that supposedly neither member of the "Foreign Relations Department" could speak English. Also, that one had a date with an American nurse for that night. How did that come about with the language barrier? I thanked Zukov for the gifts and proceeded on to my next lecture.

Immediately after returning to SAM from my "educational" trip, I contacted the OSI (Office of Special Investigation). It was Air Force policy that if any service member is addressed and spoken to by a foreign national, that must be reported to the OSI office at your home base immediately after your return. I gave the agent there the particulars of the "chance" meeting, the gist of the conversation, and made copies of the name and address slips I had received. I also showed them the space flight pins that Dr. (?) Zukov had given me. Three weeks went by with no further contact and it appeared to be a closed subject.

One afternoon, while addressing the pile of paperwork on my desk, my secretary, Mary, rapped on my door, entered, and announced that I had a visitor, a Mr. Brant. I didn't recall knowing a Mr. Brant, but told her to send him in. Mr. Brant entered, looking very fit and trim, dressed nicely in a dark blue suit. He waited until Mary had closed the door behind her and then stepped forward extending his hand. I reached out to shake it but, instead, found a white business card being pushed into my hand. It read, "Clinton B. Brant, Special Agent—Federal Bureau of Investigation, Ft. Worth, Texas." I wondered what a Ft. Worth agent was doing in San Antonio. A very pleasant man, he said he understood I had met three Russians in Washington, DC. Over the next ten minutes I had told the whole story of the Washington contact. He took a few notes. Again, I made copies of the address papers and names of the Russians. He asked if I had gotten any of the photos they had promised to send me. When I told him I hadn't, he asked, "Why don't you write and ask for them?" I said I would do that, though by this time I had figured I'd never see them at all.

There were periodic foreign language courses given at my base. They were usually one-week courses. Almost magically there was a course in Russian coming up the following week and I enrolled in it. Within one week, I could read and pronounce the Cyrillic alphabet words. I could even print them. But writing in Russian would take a bit of practice. I had a Russian *Common Phrases* book and a Russian/English Dictionary. The vocabulary would always be a "work in progress." Nevertheless, I had a start, and the following week, July 13 to be precise, I wrote a letter to Dr. Zukov. At least the beginning of it was in Russian. I sent it to the Institute of Biomedical Problems.

Basically it said, "Dear Comrade, how are you? I hope you are well. I am just learning Russian so I will continue in English." I asked him to give my regards to his two associates and, by the way, "How did the pictures turn out?" Could he send me copies? Again thanking him for the Soyuz pins, I concluded in Russian with (English pronunciation) "Blagodaryu vos" (thank you) and "Da Svidonya" (good-bye). I signed my name in Russian.

A full three weeks later, I received a reply from Zukov. It began, in Russian, "Good wishes to you, Comrade Colonel" then continued in very good English script. He "begged for mercy" for the long delay in answering, saying that once he returned to Russia from the US, all three of them went on a long vacation. Then he explained that the film they took in Washington was "spoiled" and the quality of the pictures "very poor." Furthermore, his two friends, Andrey and Vladimir, were not available for contact since they worked in a different area from him, so he had very little contact with them. In the envelope Zukov had enclosed a couple dozen Russian stamps, many of which were commemorative stamps from Russian space flights.

Russian stamps sent by Leonid

He wished I could visit Russia one day so he could be my host. He closed the letter wishing me "every happiness, quick promotion, and Hercules health," signing it L. Zukov. Quite interesting was the fact that between the sheets of stamps were four of the Washington photos, all very clear and crisp, in black and white. So much for the "spoiled film" and "poor quality." I called Clint and he arrived the next day. I made copies of the letter and the photos for him. He said, "Keep writing. I need to check out a few things."

On October 23 I replied to Zukov's letter, thanking him for the stamps and telling him I had deciphered all the script on the space pins and the stamps. I did not comment about the pictures specifically, just that all the contents of the envelope had arrived in good condition. In my letter I enclosed a brochure about the School of Aerospace Medicine which described all of our divisions and some of the work being done within them. Then I asked him for information about the Institute for Biological Problems.

Months passed with no reply. Clint dropped by periodically to see if I had received any more mail. Then his visits became less frequent with the apparent halt in communications from Zukov. I tried another letter to Zukov. In it, I noted that I had not heard from him for some time. I also told him of a major change coming about in my life.

30

~ Have I Got A Deal For You— Part 3 ~

During this lull in international correspondence, a "head hunting" group had contacted me and paid me a visit. It seems a major U.S. chemical company, now headquartered in Manhattan, New York, was moving their head office to Dallas, Texas. They were in the market for their first Medical Director. The position needed to be filled by a physician with preventative medicine and public health knowledge, as well as being conversant in public relations and budgetary matters. The main goal of the position was to establish a preventative medicine program for all company employees at all sites—and there were multiple site in the U.S., Canada, Mexico, Saudi Arabia, and Singapore. The company was also looking for medical input into a new, computerized health monitoring program they were constructing. This program, once completed, would associate data from each employee's annual medical examination with the department in which he or she worked. It further listed all the chemicals that were then being used in that department and industrial hygiene sampling data revealing the potential airborne levels of these chemicals to which the employees possibly could be exposed.

Finally, the program would provide the analyst with the length of time each employee had been working in that department and additional information about the previous departments in which they had worked. The bottom line was to create a program which would assure the company that no ill effects in their employees were coming from work-related exposure. Additionally, knowing what potential medical problems could arise from over-exposure, if any, each employee's laboratory work needed to be designed to detect any early signs of excess chemical exposure.

That was not a small task.

The "recruiting agency" knew more about me than I did myself. Their pitch to me was this:

> You are now 48 years old. You have 23 years of active duty service and, therefore, are eligible for full retirement benefits from the Air Force. You are no longer on flying status, which we know you loved, nor are you practicing medicine for which you went through all your medical training and residency. If you are considering a second career, now is the time, and the age, to pursue it. You would be a company "Director" with appropriate compensation for that level, and you'd also be eligible for the "upper management bonus program." Additionally, the move would be easy, San Antonio to Dallas.

Their points were pretty hard to argue against. To a great degree, aerospace medicine is occupational medicine. I was board certified in one and board eligible in the other. I had my Master's in Public Health and years of experience dealing with people and budgets. I asked how they came to know about me and my background, and they told me that my name had been given to them by another Air Force physician who had gone through the same training as I. He had retired from the Air Force and they had placed him as the Medical Director of Arco Petroleum in California. *Thanks, Bob!*

I needed a few days to think about it and to talk it over with the family. Moreover, I wanted to be "above board" with the Air Force. They had been very good to me. I made an appointment to see my boss, a two star general. Sitting in his office, I went through all the information the "recruiter" had laid out for me. Then I asked, "What do you think?" "Well, Larry," he said, "we'd certainly like you to stay. We can't meet the financial side of the offer you received, so the decision will have to be yours. I hope, however, to make it a little more difficult for you. I am going to show you a piece of paper, and if you ever tell anyone you saw it, I'm going to call you a liar." He reached into the left upper drawer of his desk and pulled out a single sheet of paper. There were just a few names on the sheet, one of which was mine. The paper was the nominations list of the upcoming Brigadier General promotions for the USAF Medical Corps. Talk about pressure! I asked, "If I was to take that promotion, what kind of time commitment would I be taking on?" He said, "Probably four to five years."

Job hunting at age 52 or 53 would be a lot tougher. Two days later I told the general of my decision. I thought I could do well in the position offered and would enjoy the challenge of the chemical company goals. I put in my papers with a retirement date of May 1980. I had one month's leave time coming and, as the chemical company needed me ASAP, I actually began work with them on April 1.

So my short letter to Zukov related that around April I would be moving to Dallas for my new position. I threw in only a few lines about the nature of the job and that I would be with a major chemical company. I also gave him my new work address. Almost immediately I received a belated "Happy New Year" postcard from Zukov. On the card he wished me well and informed me that the big delay in correspondence might be attributed to the fact that he had been transferred to a new position in Amman, Jordan.

The card was dated 23 February 1980. He also sent me his new work address, "Manager of the Soviet Team, Jordanian Electric Power Co. Ltd." At the bottom of the card, apparently as an afterthought, he wrote "Do not send mail to me titled Dr. Zukov." So much for being a physician. Two more letters followed in the next few months, some saying, "Why haven't I heard from you?" and also telling me he had sent several letters to me. Interestingly, one of those two letters was postmarked from Washington DC. Another of his long-delayed letters also arrived, telling me he was moving to Jordan. I was getting pretty confused by all this. One more postcard arrived before my move to Dallas, saying that his wife, especially, was enjoying the "Oriental-Western" pattern of life in Jordan, and she loved the "Western music". I have no idea what that was all about.

My military retirement was a grand affair. My boss, General Ord, had presented me with a beautiful plaque from my ten divisions, at a previous, less formal ceremony.

(top) Surgeon General Paul Myers presents Larry with Legion of Merit; (middle left) A wall box with Legion of Merit medal and other memorabilia; (middle right) Maj. General Ord presents plaque from 10 divisions of SAM; (bottom left) Legion of Merit certificate

General Shafer had retired, so the new Surgeon General of the Air Force flew down from Washington D.C. to officiate at my formal retirement ceremony. He spoke on my behalf, expressing much appreciation for my contributions to the Air Force, and bestowed on me the Presidential "Legion of Merit" medal.

In the SAM Auditorium, about one thousand people attended the ceremony. My children, now mostly all grown, had front row seats. The Air Force band played before and after the ceremonies. There was a big reception at the Officers Club along with a lot of handshaking and a few tears, mostly my own. I had lost my Government house and staff car. Good Lord, I was a civilian again! And now every morning I'd have to make a decision about what to wear!

I hadn't invited Mr. Brant, and with my departure from the Air Force, I assumed our relationship was a thing of the past. The transition to my new position went smoothly and there was a lot for me to learn about the chemical business—and a lot to re-learn about toxicology. There were five plants to visit in Texas; four were production plants, one for research. Canada had three plants and there were five more in Mexico. About a month after I started in Dallas, the new Commander at SAM asked me to come down for a day to attend the unveiling and mounting of a 24 x 36 inch hand-painted portrait of me. It was to be installed in the Commander's Hallway of the Education Building. This was traditional, and I believe it is still hanging there.

Back at the Chemical Company Headquarters, my large staff (one secretary/receptionist and one chief nurse) and I sat down to brainstorm ways to improve the "wellness" of all our employees. Over the next several years, we would develop a pretty good medical program. It was one that offered participating employees every chance to improve their physical and mental health.

New portrait unveiled of past SAM commander

"The only thing that concerns me is that now the wall is completely covered and I wonder where I will hang when the time comes," commented Col. Roy L. DeHart, SAM commander.

DeHart's comment was made during a portrait unveiling ceremony here last week honoring former SAM commander, Dr. (Col., ret.) Lawrence W. Enders.

Enders retired from active duty in August 1980, after serving his last two years as SAM commander. He was no stranger to SAM or to San Antonio even before then, as he was sent immediately to the primary course in Aviation Medicine at Randolph AFB when he entered the Air Force in 1957.

The Minnesotan's assignments kept bringing him back to Texas. He was selected by NASA for training and subsequent duties as an Aeromedical Flight Controller for the Mercury and Gemini projects with primary physician duties during the Gemini, 4, 5, 6, 7 and 9 missions.

After being one of the pioneers involved with the manned space flight, Enders was assigned to the Aeromedical Consultation Service at SAM, where he was the medical evaluator of astronaut candidates for NASA.

A stint in Thailand broke up his assignments here. When he returned to SAM he became the Chief of the Flight Medicine Branch and Consultant Service, where he remained until 1970.

A number of different assignments kept Enders busy until he assumed command of the school in 1978.

Ender's portrait was painted by Erwin Q. Wesp, a former SAM civilian employee in the AMD graphics shop.

PORTRAIT DEDICATION -- Dr. (Col., ret.) Lawrence W. Enders casts an appraising glance at his portrait which was unveiled in ceremonies last week.

Portrait of Commander, Colonel Lawrence J. Enders still hangs at SAM

Two years later, our progress had allowed us to hire a fitness manager for our staff. I had a small clinic in the headquarters to treat some of the 300 people working there. I went to each plant and presented talks to the employees on preventative medicine. The bad effects of cholesterol on the cardiovascular system were just being brought to the attention of the American public. Our routine laboratory tests included cholesterol levels; not only total cholesterol, but also HDL and LDL. These values I explained in my lectures. Along that line, we supported contests between plants by displaying percentages of employees with elevated cholesterol and seeing who could lower their percentage the most. The nurses at each plant gave personal counseling to employees with abnormal values. We started the CHEF program (Company Health Education and Fitness) which provided any employee who wanted to join a local fitness center a half-price membership, with the company paying the other half.

In the meantime, I had not yet escaped my previous life. My secretary popped her head into my office one day to announce,

"There's a Clint somebody here to see you." Mr. Brant had found me again. It had been almost six months since I had seen him in San Antonio. We exchanged greetings and I said, "You must be here for a reason." He said, "Yes, we've finally completely checked out your three Russian friends." "And?" I inquired. "Mr. Zukov is a Captain in the KGB. Mr. Zelnikov is also KGB, as is Mr. Kruzovkin, who has just been thrown out of Australia, persona non gratis, for being an industrial spy. We'd like you to keep writing to Zukov." I mentioned that I hadn't heard from him for quite a while but that I'd give it another shot.

I used a double-barreled approach. I wrote to General Oleg Gazenko, head of the Russian Aerospace Medical Institute, and sent a newsy letter to Zukov in Jordan, mentioning all the chemicals we made at the Company. At least some part of that worked, as several weeks later I received a letter from Zukov. In it, he apologized profusely for not replying to my earlier letter and mentioned that General Gezenko had written to him to remind him of "his manners" in corresponding with me.

I don't know if, in General Gezenko's correspondence to Zukov, he mentioned that I had asked about Zukov's whereabouts and that I had not heard from him for some time. Whatever worked, right? Now I had more mail than I needed. The Russian General wrote to me explaining that Zukov had been transferred to Jordan, and he also invited me, though not formerly, to come by his Institute whenever I could, as I would be welcome there.

Zukov and I exchanged several more letters, mostly light conversation. But occasionally, mixed in with the rest of the letter, there were small indications of how we thought about more serious things. I was also wondering if Zukov had any idea that I knew he was KGB. As a little test, in one of my letters I mentioned that I had a nice gun collection which included several foreign handguns but that I'd love to get hold of a Russian Graz Burya to add to it. I told him that if he was here in the U.S., I would take him shooting with me. The Graz Burya, at that time, was the standard handgun issued to most KGB agents. Zukov didn't even flinch. In his reply he stated he'd love to go shooting with me—and that he could "probably make some showing off." I think he knew.

I thought I'd jiggle Gezenko's cage a little, as well. In my reply to his letter, I thanked him for his invitation and blamed a heavy workload at my company for declining to come visit "at this time." I also mentioned to the general that I was aware of a new 1.3 million pound a year ethylene plant that was being built in Tonish, Western Siberia. It was to be completed in 1983. I asked him what the Russian Government employee exposure standards were at the plant site. I was surprised when he sent them to me.

Zukov and I continued our correspondence. I sent him a pocket knife bearing our Company logo. He was very appreciative and again informed me how much he and his family enjoyed Amman and the more Western styles. Then there were no letters for a while. I wrote twice more before his replies began again. He told me he was surprised that his letter to me had not gotten through. He commented on his sadness at the fact that the Russians and the U.S. were not sharing their space research data. He told me of his family's dreams, in that they would love to be able to travel more. The next letter had part of a page missing. It looked like the envelope had been opened and the sheet was torn. I wrote back to him and told him about that. His reply was "Yes, *something* seems to be interfering with our communication. Most probably, security officers here disliked the letter."

Zukov's last letter to me arrived on May 5. In it, he mentioned that he was 34 years old and had lived a "controversial life". "We do not attend church and are non-believers. Probably we will change our minds with time." He again mentioned Jordan and how fascinating it was. His closing was, "Larry, is it possible for you to get a picture of Tom Stafford, signed by him, for me?

Back in Moscow I used to collect photos of the cosmonauts and astronauts. I hope this letter reaches you and finds you and your family in good health and joyful mood. Your friend, Leonid Zukov."

I haven't heard from him since my letters were never answered but he is not forgotten. In my memorabilia book I do have, safely put away, a very nice 8 x 10 inch color photo of Tom Stafford, in full space suit. On the photo is written, *"To Leonid Zukov, with my best wishes, General Tom Stafford, Gemini VI, Gemini IX, Apollo X and Apollo/Soyuz."* Tom was glad to do it for me. But it remains undelivered. You may be wondering, what's the point of that whole story? The answer is, "I don't know." It's just the way it happened, and the FBI and I still have all the letters, all the pins, all the stamps, and all the photos. Just a little intrigue.

31

~ Doctor Who? ~

There was another little piece of life's surprises still waiting for me. Friends of mine from the Carrollton area, a suburb of Dallas, were going to San Antonio for some reason. Knowing I had been commander of SAM, they decided to take a tour of Brooks AFB. They called me and asked, "What should we try to see while there?" They also wanted to see if, in fact, my portrait actually did exist and was hung there somewhere. Skeptics!

I briefed them on some of the things that might interest them. There was Hangar 17, loaded with space memorabilia. Then, there were the human centrifuge, altitude chambers and other things. I asked them if they would inquire about my old "office visitor," Dr. Strughold. I told them that all the staff there knew him so it shouldn't be difficult tracking him down. Also, I suggested they visit the very large library there bearing his name.

It was a month or so before I saw my friends again. They told me that they did, indeed, see all of the exciting things I had listed for them . . . and, yes, my portrait was hanging in the Education Building. They were quite impressed with the tour. Then I asked, "And what about my old friend, Dr. Strughold? Did you see him?" That curbed their enthusiastic chatter, and they said, "The tour guide said there was no Dr. Strughold there. He had died a few years before and now no one spoke about him." I didn't quite understand what they were saying and asked, "Well, you saw his library, didn't you?" "No. There was no Hubertus Strughold Aerospace Medical Library," they replied. "There is only the USAF Aerospace Medical Library." "I don't get it," I said. "It's there." Obviously, something was very wrong.

Then they said, "A few who knew of him did not care to speak about him." I asked why and they handed me several pieces of paper from their computer search. I glanced at the papers and felt only disbelief and sadness. One of the papers was headlined "Project Paperclip! Nazi scientists who performed human experimentation are in the US." Dr. Strughold's picture was at the top of the article. From Wikipedia, I encountered this:

> *Identifying Dr. Strughold as the Father of Aerospace Medicine and Director of the Department of Space Medicine at the USAF School of Aerospace Medicine—the Aeromedical Library was renamed because documents from the Nuremburg War Crimes Tribunal linked Strughold to medical experiments in which inmates from Dachau concentration camp were tortured and killed.*

Another report stated:

> "Library won't be named for Nazi scientist," Air Force assures Anti-defamation League."

From the Jewish Bulletin:

> "Name of scientist nixed from library due to Nazi past."

And there were several more. I was shocked and more than a little heart-broken. Was this the lonely, kind old man who visited me so often? The same one who brought me those wonderful gifts, asked me to "preface" his book, and whose latest two books I keep with the inscriptions to me personalized by the "Father" himself? Was this the man who bestowed upon me the picture of W.C. Roentgen's first X-ray from Wurtzburg University? And, finally, what about the "moon rock" he gave me? Did "serendipity" pull a fast one on me this time? I think it may have!

32

~ Tales Of Trials ~

I spent a lot of time that evening thinking about things. In the beginning of this book, I said something to the effect, "We all think we are in control of our lives." Obviously, that's not always so. Realistically, we learn that everyone we know, almost everyone with whom we come in contact, and everything we see or experience in some way shapes or re-shapes the course of our lives. And then, some place within it all, serendipity slips in to add to or change that course.

I was reminded of my War College days and the lectures about "treaties" and "International Law," and that most of us, especially governments, do what is in their "best interest" at the time. Of course, the CIA knew everything there was to know about Dr. Strughold before they "acquired" him. They also knew that this man had the knowledge we needed to get the "first" man to the moon. The end justifies the means, right? It's that simple. Rules, treaties, laws, morals are allegedly what we should abide by—when they are in our "best interest." I don't know what the whole truth is about Dr. Strughold; I only know what I saw. Maybe he was a repenting, tired old man. I don't know.

Back at the Chemical Company, we continued to work at establishing a solid, comprehensive medical program. Traveling to each city where we had a production plant, I negotiated with local drug and alcohol recovery centers to give us reasonable group rates for employees who may have need of their services. Local physicians in those same towns were contracted to give emergency care to our plant employees. The plant nurse, in the case of an accident or other medical emergency, would call the local physician first and then me, in Dallas. On visits, I provided the local doctors with the type of information they would need to handle problems in case of a chemical spill. We established fitness programs at each plant, and I would drop by the plants on a bi-monthly basis to give talks on preventative medicine to the entire plant population. I usually visited the Canadian and Mexican plants quarterly.

Things never got dull, and strange events did not seem to avoid me.

If you lived in Texas in the '70's, you would have heard of the Cullen Davis Murder Trials. A very prominent Ft. Worth figure, Mr. Cullen Davis, was heir to an oil fortune and already worth more than 100 million dollars. He was on trial for his life. The following information was taken from a conglomeration of newspaper articles and a great deal from a book co-written by Steven Naifeh and Gregory White Smith called *"Final Justice."* It gave detailed accounts of interviews, court records, and trial details concerning the alleged crimes attributed to one Mr. Cullen Davis.

> *Cullen had moved out of his Fort Worth mansion, allowing his estranged wife, Priscilla, to live there. She was, allegedly, a somewhat wild partner and a "man's woman." On the evening of August 2, 1976, Priscilla had been out partying with her lover, had run into some other friends and invited them all to "her" house for some late drinks. Priscilla's twelve-year-old daughter had been left home alone. When the group arrived at the mansion, Priscilla and her lover, Stan Farr, entered the house first. The two other couples, following in their own car, were a few minutes behind them. As Priscilla and Stan headed for the kitchen, a small man, wearing a woman's black wig, stepped out of the shadows with a handgun and fired several times. Four shots hit, and killed, Stan Farr while another round hit Priscilla in the chest. As she fell, she recognized the shooter as her husband, Cullen*

Davis. She called out, "Cullen, what are you doing?" The perpetrator then ran out the front door, directly into the other arriving guests who knew Davis. He began firing at them, hitting three and killing one of them. They also shouted at him, calling out his name. And then he was gone. After the police arrived, they found the body of the 12-year-old girl, shot to death, in the basement of the house. Cullen Davis had been identified as the shooter by four people, all of whom knew him by sight.

Cullen was arrested and charged with the murders. Davis hired one of the most famous celebrity lawyers in Texas, Richard "Race Horse" Haynes. After a series of preliminary court hearings, although the charge of multiple murder remained, Haynes managed to get Davis released on bail, pending trial. The media had a field day! So much that the lawyers managed to get the trial moved from Ft. Worth to Amarillo. Through means only known to Haynes, the word was spread around that Priscilla was an extremely "loose" woman and a money-grubbing drunk and druggie. Even before the trial ever started, she was the "slut woman" of Texas. Davis' legal team did a masterful job on the members of the Amarillo court and the jury which was loaded with "good ole boys."

The trial, which ended up being more of a morals trial about Priscilla than a murder trial about Cullen Davis, lasted about fifteen months before the jury reconvened in the court room with their verdict of "not guilty—on all counts." (That slut woman got what she had comin'.) There was a huge party after the acquittal. All of Davis' team celebrated, and before the party was over, they were joined by the judge and several of the jurors. Oh, and the bailiff was there as well. "Race Horse" Haynes celebrated by grabbing a guitar and singing "The Ballad of Cullen Davis."

In June, prior to the end of the trial, Priscilla had sought a decree by another judge, who awarded her "$5,000 a month for the rest of her life." The cash was to be taken directly from the accounts of Ken Davis Industries, side-stepping Cullen Davis himself. Cullen was furious. Additionally, the judge had awarded the monthly payment indefinitely. Cullen dealt with a somewhat less-than-scrupulous associate to "get him a gun." Furthermore, Cullen guaranteed him a $25,000 payment if he would kill the judge, his wife, and several others who had made charges against him at the murder trial. The potential assassin backed off from the long list of victims but agreed to kill the judge for the $25,000. However, before the plans for the killing of the judge could be carried out, the assassin got cold feet. Wanting to be rid of his involvement, he went to the FBI, but they persuaded him to "go along" with the contract. The FBI developed fake evidence that the contract killing had been carried out. They told the judge about the contract killing, and he also agreed to go along with a "sting" operation.

The FBI got the judge to allow for cigarette burns to be made in one of his shirts and fake blood to be painted around the holes. The judge put on the shirt and then crawled into the trunk of the "assassin's" car. A photo was taken of the "dead" judge, a proof which Cullen had demanded before payment. Cullen agreed to meet the assassin in a parking lot and make payment pending the "proof" of the killing. The FBI posted a surveillance van next to the prescribed meeting place and audio-wired the contractor's car and the man himself. They also had cameras looking through the "one way" window of their van to film the whole exchange of payment. Indeed, the FBI did film the money transfer and recorded the conversation between Cullen and the "shooter." And Cullen was rearrested. "Race Horse" had his client back!

At the hearing, Davis pleaded "Not Guilty." The second trial began in Houston. Jury selection took "forever" but the trial did, finally, begin. The prosecution presented the tapes and the conversation between Davis and the assassin was heard. On those tapes was Cullen's request to have five different people killed. Haynes tore the "gunman" apart with facts and accusations which completely shredded his credibility. The whole story was so twisted that in the end it was the contention of the defense that the original $25,000 had been Priscilla's money, given to the shooter to kill Cullen Davis, and that the assassin had given the $25,000 to Cullen to hold for him. Further, the filming of the money transfer was simply Cullen giving him his own money back. It was also their contention that in the recorded conversation, Cullen's comments of "Good" and "Okay" (when told the judge was dead) did not constitute a direct admission that he had ordered the "killing."

The trial stretched to January 1979, and by that time the jury was totally confused as to who did what to whom. They were totally exasperated from hearing all the claims and counterclaims. Their first verdict ballot, in the jury room, was eight for "guilty" and four for "not guilty." Their deliberations went on for several days. On the sixth day, Deliberation #14, the count was still the same. As a result, the judge declared the whole mess a "mistrial" and dismissed the case. Legally, there could be another trial—but would there be? Well, sometime later there was—this time in Ft. Worth. The result of that one? Acquittal! Cullen Davis was a free man but no longer a multimillionaire. He did, however, marry his girlfriend of three years, Karen Master.

The courts, lawyers, and suspected payoffs exhausted his money. Legal fees, foreclosures, civil lawsuits, and bankruptcy took whatever little was left. Part of that was a $21 million lawsuit brought against Davis by Priscilla for damages to her and her dead daughter, Andrea. Again came the confusing testimonies and again a mistrial was declared. Davis was now virtually bankrupt, with less than $2 million to his name, but with $860 million in liabilities. Following his financial downfall, Davis found God! He gave several prayer meetings at large arenas in the Dallas/Ft. Worth area and sold some bibles. James Robison considered Davis his #1 disciple. Cullen began preaching against the theory of evolution. He also gave seminars on spiritual welfare, but these, of course, brought him very little money.

By now I am sure you're asking yourself . . . what has all this to do with Lawrence J. Enders? Let me answer that for you. At the Chemical Company, I was sitting in my office on the fourth floor when Sue, the company's receptionist in the lobby, called me and said, "Dr. Enders, there's a Mr. Davis here to see you." "I don't know a Mr. Davis," I told her. She whispered into the telephone, "It's a Mr. Cullen Davis." The name woke me up, and I asked her to send him up to my office.

Cullen Davis walked into my office, extended his hand, and looked me straight in the eye. I suspect he was checking for some sign of recognition. I hoped I didn't project any. "What can I do for you, Mr. Davis?" I asked. "It's what I can do for you that's important!" he replied with great confidence. "Let me show you something."

He began to unpack a rather heavy case. What he was about to demonstrate to me was his latest financial endeavor involving a protective hand cream. He took from his case a glass container of concentrated hydrochloric acid, an empty beaker, and a piece of very heavy aluminum foil. He laid the piece of foil on top of the empty beaker. With his finger he made a small indentation in the foil that would allow it to hold, possibly, a half ounce of fluid. Into this indentation he poured several milliliters of the hydrochloric acid. It took only a second for the acid to send up some vapor and burn completely through the foil. He then pulled from his case a small bottle of his hand lotion. He poured about half an ounce of the lotion into his left hand and rubbed it in for about fifteen or twenty seconds. After a moment, he asked me to feel his hand. I did, and found it to be smooth and dry.

He proceeded to take the same bottle of hydrochloric acid and poured about half an ounce into the palm of his left hand, which he had previously rubbed with his lotion. Then he just stood there, looking at me. Apparently he was experiencing no discomfort from a hand full of acid. Shortly thereafter, he dumped the liquid from his hand onto the foil and it went into the beaker, taking a bit more of the foil with it. He washed his hands with water from another beaker and then let me examine his hand. It was a very impressive demonstration. His point was, of course, that we should consider purchasing his product for our plant employees to help protect them from any corrosive chemicals.

I told him that his demo was pretty impressive, but, as the Medical Director, I had no purchasing power for safety equipment, but I would be happy to set up a time for a second demonstration for our safety and industrial hygiene managers. I believe that some of the products could be purchased for areas where our employees would benefit from that kind of protection. Mr. Davis left a relatively happy man.

Shortly after his departure, Sue, our receptionist, came to my office, an emotional mess. Almost breathless she said, "Dr. Enders, that man scared me to death!" I asked her why she was so scared, and she said, "Because I was so nervous with him sitting there, waiting for you. I kept glancing at him, and then he slowly walked up to my desk. He put his face within inches of mine and whispered, 'You know me, don't you?' Dr. Enders, I almost peed my pants!"

I have a very interesting Christmas Card in my memorabilia collection, one that wished me "a full year of happiness and success" from Karen and Cullen Davis. I'm glad he gave me a year. Allegedly, he didn't give some other people that long.

BOOKS

Sunday, October 24, 1993 — The Dallas Morning News

Taking a new look at an old murder case

Cullen Davis

FINAL JUSTICE: The True Story of the Richest Man Ever Tried for Murder
By Steven Naifeh and Gregory White Smith (NAL/Dutton, $24)

By Dan Malone

In the late 1970s, multimillionaire Cullen Davis was accused of shooting to death his 12-year-old stepdaughter, wounding his estranged wife and killing her lover at his mansion in southwest Fort Worth. He was subsequently charged with a failed murder-for-hire plot to kill the judge presiding over his spectacularly messy divorce.

The pile of criminal and civil cases filed against Mr. Davis was ultimately resolved in his favor: No jury voted to hold him responsible for the deaths. But the protracted litigation that dogged Mr. Davis for more than a decade nevertheless raised troubling questions that time has not adequately answered.

Could a man of vast wealth and
Please see MURDER on Page 9J.

Murder trial raised hard questions

IT'S A REAL PLEASURE AT THIS HOLIDAY TIME TO SAY

"THANK YOU"

AS WE WISH YOU A FULL YEAR OF HAPPINESS AND SUCCESS

KAREN and CULLEN DAVIS

The case of Cullen Davis

33

~ Causes & Correlations ~

We had a very large production plant where some of the employees had begun to call one unit "the Cancer Unit." Why? Because out of the twelve people that worked there, six of them had been diagnosed with cancer. Naturally, management was quite upset with the rumors and stories coming from that location. I reviewed all the medical examinations on the six "cancer" employees. That included all their lab work, medical histories, physical data, and potential exposure data. I could certainly understand the concern of the workers. Cancer in six out of twelve employees was certain to give rise to questions of safety. The problem is that rumors are often founded on partial information and, often, erroneous information. But cancer is a terrible disease, and the employees needed some answers. Can it be caused by contact with some chemicals? Yes, it can.

My review of the six employees revealed this: One employee was an older man with prostate cancer that had been diagnosed years before he came to the company. Another was a middle-aged woman with breast cancer. A third person had skin cancer. One, a heavy smoker, had lung cancer and had worked in the unit only three weeks before his diagnosis. There was another woman with uterine cancer. The last case was of an older gentleman, an avid pipe-smoker, who developed a cancerous lesion on the lip where he held his pipe.

There were six cases of cancer, no two alike, at very different locations and very different induction times. But all the employees heard was "six cancer diagnoses in one unit," and they assumed a "cause and effect" relationship. It was time for a short course in "Cause and Effect" versus "Correlation." They were seeing a correlation!

I flew down to the plant and one evening gave a short course to the employees' families. First, I explained what "induction time" is—that's the time that transpires between when the cancer causing agent is first encountered and when the cancer is detected or becomes evident in the patient. Almost every cancer has an induction time of a year or more. So if you display symptoms and a cancer is diagnosed today, it actually began some significant time before. Genetics play a major part in susceptibility to contracting cancer. And as for causal agents, looking at the six cases, there was no one agent that would have caused all of those different cancers.

Still, some employees were worried—six cancers in one unit. That was a correlation, and I explained correlation as follows:

> I drew two graphs. On one graph I put children's ages on the bottom horizontal line. On the left (vertical) line, I put the number of children whose parents had bought them their first bike. At age one, almost no bikes. Ages two to three, a few bikes. By age five, a reasonable number of bikes, etc., so that, by age 10, about 50% of the children had bikes.
>
> On the other graph, again I put age on the bottom line, and the number of childhood leukemia cases on the left vertical line. Again, at age one, very few cases; ages two to three, a few cases. Age five, several cases, etc., so that by age 10, there were a significant number of cases. I drew the curves on both charts, then laid the graph with the leukemia curve over the graph with the bicycle curve. They were almost identical.

> Then, I said to the audience, "There you are. These curves match almost perfectly. So, it's very obvious that buying a child a bike causes leukemia, right?" The room was very quiet. I continued, "This is correlation. It is NOT cause and effect." Now they understood. Case closed.

We produced enough potent chemicals to keep the medical staff on their toes. I co-authored two epidemiological studies on exposure versus health, and I spoke at occupational health meetings. There were good years and there were bad years; good bosses and bad bosses. One of my bosses disliked doctors. His brother was a doctor and it was said that he hated him. After his physical exam, I tried to counsel him on a serious finding, but he would rather die than take my advice or the medication I had procured for him. Some years later he did die from the condition I was trying to control for him—and it was controllable.

There were trips to Canada and Mexico to do formal inspections of medical facilities and to assure management that all the rules and regulations were being followed. But after seventeen years with the company and a quadruple coronary by-pass, I felt I had just about done my fair share of work.

By this time, all the kids were grown and gone.

34

~ Did You Find the "Yet" Yet? ~

My wife and I decided to settle in a small condo overlooking the Atlantic Ocean in Jacksonville Beach, Florida. Now we had time to travel, and travel we did. We visited some thirty countries over the next ten years. But one can't travel all the time and the "work bug" bit me again. But not quite as hard. So for four years I taught the advanced course in Anatomy and Physiology (called A&P 2) for pre-med and nursing students at Florida Community College. Only 24 students were allowed in each class, and I have never had so much fun. And neither did the students! We all discovered that teaching, learning, and enjoyment can be mixed. The Associate Dean sat in on several of my classes and couldn't believe the relaxed relationship we all had, always courteous but appropriately intimate. I went over each exam with the students before a test was given. I did not give them the exact questions but told them to what the questions referred.

For example, if my test question was going to be "List the four valves in the heart in order of blood flow," I might say before class, "You must be able to track the blood through the heart and know all the structures it passes through, including all chambers and valves." On most of my exams, I would give extra points for bonus questions. I was also a bit of a "trickster." Invariably, on my final laboratory exam, I would assign two students per fetal pig. They had to dissect the pig and find, to my satisfaction, the fifty organs or structures I had listed on a sheet. I also told them there would be a two-point extra bonus for anyone who could locate the *yet* in the pig. "The what?" they'd ask. "The *yet*, "I'd say." Better get started." They would spend two hours dissecting the pigs and logging and identifying all the items on my list, with the exception of the *yet*. No one ever found the *yet*. Time was up . . . the exam was ended.

"Has anyone found the *yet*?" I'd ask. No one. They all gave up. "Okay, Dr. Enders, where is the *yet*?" And I would have to say, "I don't know. I was hoping you would have found it." They would look at me and ask what made me think any such thing as a *yet* actually existed? I'd say, "It must exist. It was in the paper. I read a story a few months ago about a woman who had been shot five years earlier, and the story finished by saying—'and the bullet is in her *yet*'." It always took a few minutes to sink in, amidst moans and groans, of course.

Then I would tell them, "You have all looked so hard. I have never seen pigs so completely dissected in my life. So all of you will get the two extra points." That brought on smiles and cheers. Amazingly, I did that same thing for four years and no one ever told anyone in the subsequent classes.

I retired again, and this time for the last time. Maybe.

We have lots of time to relax now, and we still travel at least once a year. For me there is time to evaluate my trip through "life" and consider the twists and turns that serendipity afforded me. Most amazing were the number of unique people with whom I had contact.

Looking at all my decisions, were my "rights" always right and were my "wrongs" always wrong? Not by a long shot! But even the "wrong" choices I made were the ones I believed, at the time, that I should have made. Each of us is different . . . special . . . unique. We are no two alike. We are like snowflakes or fingerprints.

There will always and forever be only one of each of us. We are, you are, the original—no "copies" possible. Our "uniqueness" does not always make us popular, and there are so many travelers on the "most traveled" road in this life. Oscar Wilde once said, *"My great mistake, the fault for which I can't forgive myself, is that one day I ceased my obstinate pursuit of my own originality."* We may not be able to choose the parents to whom we are born, or, indeed, where we are born. We may not be able to choose how or when we will die.

But we can all choose how we live!

Well!—guess what? After hunting unsuccessfully for years, I just recently, and quite accidentally of course, found out that Leonid Zukov is still alive. And I know where he is. I wonder if he'd still like to have that photo of Tom Stafford? I think I should try to get in touch with him.

Serendipity!!

Acknowledgments

Very special thanks to my good friend, Warren Walters... who gave precious time to take my handwritten and taped "life" stories and put them in some semblance of order on his computer. His deciphering of my scribble was itself a wonder. Also, his terrific "editing-as-he-went" and wonderful Aussie humor helped keep me grounded.

To my dedicated friend, Mary Ellen Gardner... my most sincere appreciation for pushing me "over the edge" of hesitation about relating these events. I also give her my very warmest thanks for her hours of detailed editing and word-smithing efforts. I have an additional indebtedness to Mary Ellen for contacting the local news-writer, who ultimately videotaped a specific segment of my story for the Veterans' Historical Society.

To my wonderful daughter, Kristine Marie Enders Doyle, Director of Strategic Communications at The University of Texas Health Science Center at San Antonio... my love and thanks for volunteering to do the layout and design and ensuring that all the pieces came together into a viable book format.

Last, but not least... my thanks, love, and deep appreciation to my lovely wife, Janet. She is my champion and biggest fan. She also endured countless days and nights of abandonment while I isolated myself in our study drafting and redrafting text, downloading pictures, and wracking my memory. I also appreciate her constructive critiques and editorial comments which kept me in the realm of reality.

To all the above, I give my sincere thanks for their support, enthusiasm, and labors of love in helping get my serendipitous experiences chronicled. You are all forever in my heart.

(No cameras were harmed in the filming of above portraits).

"Additionally I must not fail to acknowledge the tremendous help from Patti Smith who critiqued the final galley proof assisting with changes. My very warm thanks and appreciation."

Edwards Brothers Malloy
Thorofare, NJ USA
August 24, 2012